Proceedings of the
11th Paul D. Converse Symposium

11ᵗʰ proceedings of the Paul D. Converse Symposium

edited by

David M. Gardner and
Frederick W. Winter

of the University of Illinois at Champaign

Proceedings Series AMERICAN MARKETING ASSOCIATION

250 South Wacker Drive • Chicago, Illinois 60606 • (312)648-0536

Library of Congress CIP Data

Paul D. Converse Symposium (11th, 1981, University of Illinois
   at Urbana-Champaign)
   Proceedings of the 11th Paul D. Converse Symposium.

   (Proceedings series)
   1. Marketing--Congresses. I. Gardner, David Morgan.
II. Winter, Rick. III. Title. IV. Series: Proceedings series
(American Marketing Association)
HF5411.P38 1981   658.8   81-22920
ISBN 0-87757-155-4   AACR2

                                  130/1000/582

TABLE OF CONTENTS

Foreword   vii

Product Differentiation and Market Segmentation:
Another Look
    Wendell Smith   1

Demand Criteria for Normative Market Segmentation
Theory: A Retrospective View
    Henry Assael   8

Market Segmentation: A Review of Its Problems
and Promise
    Frederick W. Winter   19

The Physics and the Metaphysics of Marketing
    Robert Bartels   30

On A Metatheory of Social Behavior
    James M. Carman   36

Bartels' Metatheory of Marketing: A Perspective
    Shelby D. Hunt and Kenneth A. Hunt   50

Consumer Behavior: A Critical Assessment
    James F. Engel   59

Teaching and Researching Consumer Behavior:
Reflections on the Contributions of a Pioneering
Work
    Donald H. Granbois   70

James F. Engel: Twenty Years of Contributions
to Consumer Behavior
    W. Wayne Talarzyk and Roger D. Blackwell   79

Consumer Attitudes and Behavior: A Theory of
Reasoned Action
    Icek Ajzen   94

Lessons Learned from a Decade of Multiattribute
Attitude Research in Marketing
    Richard J. Lutz   107

FOREWORD

The papers in this volume were presented at the Eleventh Paul D. Converse Symposium at the University of Illinois, May 11-12, 1981. On that occasion, the Paul D. Converse Awards were presented to Robert Bartels, James Engel, Martin Fishbein and Wendell Smith.

The Paul D. Converse awards, granted to persons who have made outstanding contributions to the theory or science in Marketing, was established by the American Marketing Association at its meeting in Pittsburgh, Pennsylvania, on December 29, 1946. On June 13, 1948, the Directors meeting in Washington, D.C., turned over the administration of this program to the Central Illinois Chapter of the Association.

The awards are conferred during a biennial Marketing Symposium conducted by the Department of Business Administration of the College of Commerce and Business Administration of the University of Illinois.

The awards are given for definite contributions to the theory or science in Marketing; no contribution is considered until five years after it is available to marketing students generally by publication or otherwise; and members of the staff of the University of Illinois are not eligible. The selection of award recipients is made by a national jury of scholars drawn from universities, business and government who first nominate work for consideration and then rate the contributions. A committee of the Chapter tabulates the ratings and announces the results.

Special appreciation is due to Hix Huegy and Robert Mitchell for their valuable contributions as members of the Central Illinois Chapter committee to select award winners.

This volume includes presentations by three of the four awards recipients along with critiques of the recipients' contributions by other marketing scholars.

David M. Gardner
Fredrick W. Winter

PRODUCT DIFFERENTIATION AND MARKET SEGMENTATION:
ANOTHER LOOK

Wendell Smith, University of Massachusetts

INTRODUCTION

I am honored and delighted to be invited to participate in
this symposium as the capstone of my career. Among other
things, the symposium will continue to provide confidence and
stimulus to marketing professionals who are at work in the
economy and/or in the academic community. The first Converse
Symposium, which I had the honor to attend, gave many of us an
opportunity to become acquainted with some of the outstanding
scholars in the field, and stimulated us and others to try to
follow the footsteps of Vaile, Huegy, Alexander, Grether,
Aspinwal, Converse, Alderson and many others. We are also in-
debted to the University of Illinois and its faculty for continuing to bring marketing scholars, and potential scholars,
together.

As some of you know, my emphasis over time has been on
marketing strategies; most specifically, upon a market segmentation approach; or alternatively, an effective product differentiation approach. Hence, my remarks will be organized to
identify product differentiation and market segmentation as
alternative marketing strategies.

My several years outside of the academic community, at
RCA, Alderson and Sessions and the Marketing Science Institute
contributed substantially to my understanding of various marketing strategies and procedures.

Background
About half a century (at least) ago, the work of Robinson
and Chamberlin resulted in a revitalization of economic theory.
While classical and neoclassical theory provided a useful
framework for general economic analysis, the theories of perfect competition and pure monopoly had become inadequate as
explanations of the contemporary business scene. The concept
of perfect competition assumes homogeneity among the components
of both the demand and supply sides of the market, but diversity
or heterogeneity had come to be the rule rather than the exception. This development reviews major marketing strategy
alternatives that are available to planners and merchandisers
of products in an environment characterized by imperfect
competition.

Diversity in Supply

That there is a lack of homogeneity or close similarity among the items offered to the market by individual manufacturers of various products, is obvious in almost any variety store, department store, or shopping center. In many cases the impact of this diversity is amplified by advertising and promotional activities. Today's advertising and promotion tends to emphasize appeals to selective rather than primary buying motives and to point out the distinctive or differentiating features of the advertiser's product or service offer.

The presence of differences in the sales offers made by competing suppliers produces a diversity in supply. The reasons for the presence of diversity in specific markets are many and include the following Marketing Strategies:

1. Variations in the production equipment and methods or processes used by different manufacturers of products designed for the same or similar uses. (mechanical vs. electronic, etc.)

2. Specialized or superior resources enjoyed by favorably situated manufacturers.

3. Unequal progress among competitors in design, development, and improvement of products.

4. The inability of manufacturers in some industries to eliminate product variations even through the application of quality control techniques.

5. Variations in producers' estimates of the nature of market demand with reference to such matters as price sensitivity, color, material, or package size.

Because of these and other factors, both planned and uncontrollable differences may exist in the products of an industry. As a result, sellers make different appeals in support of their marketing efforts. So much for diversity in supply.

Diversity or Variations in Consumer Demand

Under present-day conditions of imperfect competition, marketing managers are generally responsible for selecting the overall marketing strategy, or combination of strategies, best suited to a firm's requirements at any particular point in time. The strategy selected may consist of a program designed to bring about the convergence of individual market demands for a variety of products upon a single or limited offering to the market. This is often accomplished by the achievement of

2

product differentiation through advertising and promotion. In
this way, variations in the demands of individual consumers are
minimized or brought into line by means of effective use of
appealing product claims designed to make a satisfactory volume
of demand converge upon the product or product line being promoted. This strategy was once believed to be essential as the
marketing counterpart to standardization and mass production in
manufacturing because of the rigidities imposed by production
cost considerations.

In some cases, however, the marketer may determine that it
is better to accept divergent demand as a market characteristic
and to adjust product lines and marketing strategy accordingly.
This implies ability to merchandise to a heterogeneous market
by emphasizing the precision with which a firm's products can
satisfy the requirements of one or more distinguishable market
segments. The strategy of product differentiation here gives
way to marketing programs based upon measurement and definition
of market differences.

Lack of homogeneity on the demand side may be based upon
different customs, desire for variety, or desire for exclusive-
ness may arise from basic differences in user needs. Some di-
vergence in demand is the result of shopping errors or stupidity
in the market. Not all consumers have the desire or the ability
to shop in a sufficiently efficient or rational manner as to
bring about selection of the most needed or most wanted goods
or services.

Diversity on the demand side of the market is nothing new
to sales management. It has always been accepted as a fact to
be dealt with in industrial markets where production to order
rather than for the market is common. Here, however, the loss
of precision in the satisfying of customer requirements that
would be necessitated by attempts to bring about convergence of
demand is often impractical and, in some cases, impossible.
However, even in industrial marketing, the strategy of product
differentiation should be considered in cases where products
are applicable to several industries and may have horizontal
markets of substantial size.

Differences Between Strategies of Differentiation and
Segmentation

Product differentiation and market segmentation are both
consistent with the framework of imperfect competition. In its
simplest terms, product differentiation is concerned with the
bending of demand to the will of supply. It is an attempt to
shift or to change the slope of the demand curve for the market
offering of an individual supplier. This strategy may also be
employed by a group of suppliers such as a farm cooperative,

the members of which have agreed to act together. It results from the desire to establish a kind of equilibrium in the market by bringing about adjustment of market demand to supply conditions favorable to the seller.

Segmentation is based upon developments on the demand side of the market and represents a rational and more precise adjustment of product and marketing effort to consumer or user requirements. In the language of the economist, segmentation is disaggregative in its effects and tends to bring about recognition of several demand schedules where only one was recognized before.

Attention has been drawn to this area of analysis by the increasing number of cases in which business problems have become soluble by doing something about marketing programs and product policies that overgeneralize both markets and marketing effort. These are situations where intensive promotion designed to differentiate the company's products was not accomplishing its objective--cases where failure to recognize the reality of market segments was resulting in loss of market position.

While successful product differentiation will result in giving the marketer a horizontal share of a broad and generalized market, equally successful application of the strategy of market segmentation tends to produce depth of market position in the segments that are effectively defined and penetrated. The differentiator seeks to secure a layer of the market cake, whereas one who employs market segmentation strives to secure one or more wedge-shaped pieces.

Many examples of market segmentation can be cited; the soap, toothpaste, and automobile industries are well-known illustrations. Similar developments exist in greater or lesser degree in almost all product areas. Introduction of a refrigerator with no storage compartment for frozen foods would be in response to the distinguishable preferences of the segment of the refrigerator market made up of home freezer owners whose frozen food storage needs had already been met.

Strategies of segmentation and differentiation may be employed simultaneously, but more commonly they are applied in sequence in response to changing market conditions. In one sense, segmentation is a momentary or short-term phenomenon in that effective use of this strategy may lead to more formal recognition of the reality of market segments through redefinition of the segments as individual markets. Redefinition may result in a swing back to differentiation.

The literature of both economics and marketing abounds in

4

formal definitions of product differentiation. From a strategy viewpoint, product differentiation is securing a measure of control over the demand for a product by advertising or promoting differences between a product and the products of competing sellers. It is basically the result of sellers' desires to establish firm market positions and/or to insulate their business against price competition. Differentiation tends to be characterized by heavy use of advertising and promotion and to result in prices that are somewhat above the equilibrium levels associated with perfectly competitive market conditions. It may be classified as a promotional strategy or approach to marketing.

Market segmentation, on the other hand, consists of viewing a heterogeneous market (one characterized by divergent demand) as a number of smaller homogeneous markets in response to differing product preferences among important market segments. It is attributable to the desires of consumers or users for more precise satisfaction of their varying wants. Like differentiation, segmentation often involves substantial use of advertising and promotion. This is to inform market segments of the availability of goods or services produced for or presented as meeting their needs with precision. Under these circumstances, prices tend to be somewhat closer to perfectly competitive equilibrium. Market segmentation is essentially a merchandising strategy, merchandising being used here in its technical sense as representing the adjustment of market offerings to consumer or user requirements.

The Emergence of the Segmentation Strategy
To a certain extent, market segmentation may be regarded as a force in the market that will not be denied. It may result from trial and error in the sense that generalized programs of product differentiation may turn out to be effective in some segments of the market and ineffective in others. Recognition of, and intelligent response to, such a situation necessarily involves a shift in emphasis. On the other hand, it may develop that products involved in marketing programs designed for particular market segments may achieve a broader acceptance than originally planned, thus revealing a basis for convergence of demand and a more generalized marketing approach. The challenge to planning arises from the importance of determining, preferably in advance, the level or degree of segmentation that can be exploited with profit.

There appear to be many reasons why formal recognition of market segmentation as a strategy have emerged. One of the most important of these is decrease in the size of the minimum efficient producing or manufacturing unit required in some product areas. American industry has also established the technical base for product diversity by gaining release from some of the rigidities imposed by earlier approaches to mass production. Hence, there is less need today for generalization of markets in response to the necessity for long production runs of identical items.

Emphasis upon the minimizing of marketing costs through self-service and similar developments tends to impose a requirement for better adjustment of products to consumer demand. The retailing structure, in its efforts to achieve improved efficiency, is tending toward providing less and less personal sales push at point of sale. This increases the premium placed by retailers upon products that are presold by their producers and are readily recognized by consumers as meeting their requirements as measured by satisfactory rates of stock turnover.

It has been suggested that the present level of discretionary buying power is productive of sharper shopping comparisons, particularly for items that are above the need level. General prosperity also creates increased willingness "to pay a little more" to get "just what I wanted."

Attention to market segmentation has also been enhanced by the recent ascendancy of product competition to a position of substantial economic importance. An expanded array of goods and services is competing for the consumer's dollar. More specifically, advancing technology is creating competition between new and traditional materials with reference to metals, construction materials, textile products, and in many other areas. While such competition is confusing and difficult to analyze in its early stages, it tends to achieve a kind of balance as various competing materials find their markets of maximum potential as a result of recognition of differences in the requirements of market segments.

Some companies are reaching the stage in their development where attention to market segmentation may be regarded as a condition or cost of growth. Their core markets have already been developed on a generalized basis to the point where additional advertising and selling expenditures are yielding diminishing returns. Attention to smaller or fringe market segments, which may have small potentials individually but are of crucial importance in the aggregate, may be indicated.

Finally, some business firms regard an increasing share of their total costs of operation as being fixed in character. The higher costs of maintaining market position in the channels of distribution illustrate this change. Total reliance upon a strategy of product differentiation under such circumstances is undesirable, since market share available as a result of

6

such a promotion-oriented approach tends to be variable over time. Exploitation of market segments, which provides for greater maximization of consumer or user satisfactions, tends to build a more secure market position and to lead to greater over-all stability.

Conclusion

Often, success in planning marketing activities requires precise utilization of both product differentiation and market segmentation as components of marketing strategy. It is the obligation of those responsible for sales and marketing administration to keep the strategy mix in adjustment with market structure at any point in time and to produce in marketing strategy at least as much dynamism as is present in the market. The ability of business to plan in this way is dependent upon the maintenance of a flow of market information that can be provided by marketing research as well as the full utilization of available techniques of cost accounting and cost analysis.

Cost information is critical because the upper limit to which market segmentation can be carried is largely defined by production cost considerations. There is a limit to which diversity in market offerings can be carried without driving production costs beyond practical limits. Similarly, the employment of product differentiation as a strategy tends to be restricted by the achievement of levels of marketing cost that are untenable. These cost factors tend to define the limits of the zone within which the employment of marketing strategies or a strategy mix dictated by the nature of the market is permissive.

It should be emphasized that while we have here been concerned with the differences between product differentiation and market segmentation as marketing strategies, they are closely related concepts in the setting of an imperfectly competitive market. The differences have been highlighted in the interest of enhancing clarity in theory and precision in practice. The emergence of market segmentation as a strategy once again provides evidence of the consumer's preeminence in the contemporary American economy and the richness of the rewards that can result from the application of science to marketing problems.

DEMAND CRITERIA FOR NORMATIVE MARKET SEGMENTATION THEORY: A RETROSPECTIVE VIEW

Henry Assael, New York University

In rereading Wendell Smith's original paper (1956), I was struck by the fact that he clearly established the basis for normative market segmentation theory. By normative market segmentation theory, I mean the demand criteria for optimally al-locating resources to alternative segments. Smith was concerned with market segmentation as a strategic alternative to the more prevalent strategy of product differentiation and as a means of improving the efficiency of marketing resource allocation. The focus in the literature on analytical methods for defining market segments (Wind 1978) sometimes loses sight of this emphasis on the allocation question and the underlying demand criteria for allocation. I thought I would try to focus on these key aspects of the concept of market segmentation by considering demand criteria for segmentation and showing how Smith's original work set the stage for subsequent approaches to market segmentation.

Specifically, I will focus on three demand criteria for segmentation: first, brand utility; second, the level of demand and third, demand elasticity. I will be using Table 1 as a basis for discussion by considering these three demand criteria, their applications in marketing, and their degree of utilization. I will then focus on response elasticity as the most important criterion for allocation across market segments and consider why use of this criterion has been so rare. I will also consider some recent challenges to the notion that grouping consumers by response elasticity represents the optimal criterion for segmentation. And finally, I will provide some thoughts as to where we are heading with these three approaches.

Before getting into these issues, let us first consider a key statement in Smith's work that underlies normative segmentation theory, namely that "Segmentation is based upon developments on the demand side of the market and represents a rational and more precise adjustment of product and marketing effort to consumer requirements." Although the statement is not startling, remember it was written in 1956 and is important for three reasons: First, it was a direct application of the emerging marketing concept; second, it represented a logical extension of the theory of imperfect competition; and third, it led to a consideration of the demand criteria for segmentation strategies that I just mentioned. Let me consider each of these three points in turn.

The relation between market segmentation and the marketing concept is clear since segmentation is directed to satisfying diverse consumer needs. The concept of market segmentation can be considered the result of the post-Korean War buyer's market. Sometime around 1953-54 it became clear that consumers were holding back on expenditures for durables despite sufficient purchasing power. This was partly due to a stocking up at the start of the Korean War and to a greater sophistication in shopping habits. It became apparent that strategies of convergence of resources on a limited number of offerings could not be sufficient to gain a competitive advantage. Moreover, by 1954, marketing institutions were sufficiently developed to permit greater diversity in product offerings. Smith defined this need for diversity in meeting consumer needs.

In addition to the marketing concept, a second underpinning of market segmentation is the theory of imperfect competition. Smith cited the works of Robinson and Chamberlin (1948, 1946) because of the importance of recognizing diversity in demand in a buyer's market. In the early 1930's Robinson and Chamberlin began moving away from the prevailing concept of an aggregate demand curve for a given product category by recognizing heterogeneity in demand and the possibility of several demand curves for separate markets. They saw that the likelihood of administered pricing rather than the market derived price of pure competition could produce the possibility of maximizing profits through price discrimination. The vehicle was pricing based on differences in demand elasticities among consumer groups. Therefore, the concept of imperfect competition recognized different demand curves at the individual consumer level. In the words of Joan Robinson:

> "The total demand of the market is made up of the demands of individual buyers. If the elasticities of demand are different, he (the manufacturer) will first divide all individual buyers into two classes such that the highest elasticity of demand in the one class is less than the least elasticity of demand in the other class." (Robinson 1948, p. 186).

Robinson then goes on to say that if after dividing consumers into two groups, there are differences in elasticities, then

> "each sub-market will be split into two on the same principle as before, the parts will again be subdivided, and so forth until the point is reached at which each sub-market consists of a

single buyer or a group of buyers whose elasticities of demand are the same." (Robinson 1948, p. 186).

Thus, Robinson has given us a very explicit criterion for defining market segments: disaggregate up to the point where elasticities of a group are the same. This criterion for maximization can easily be translated in clustering terms to mean a minimization of within group variance in elasticities and a maximization of between group variance. (See Assael and Roscoe Jr. 1976, Claycamp and Massy 1968, Frank, Massy, and Wind 1972).

Now this may be regarded as a disaggregation or aggregation criterion depending on the starting point. Given such a disaggregation of the market, Robinson also states an appropriate allocation criterion as follows:

"He (the manufacturer) can increase his profit by selling less in those markets where the elasticity of demand is less and the marginal revenue smaller, and selling more in those markets where the elasticity of demand is higher and the marginal revenue greater. He will therefore adjust his sales in such a way that the marginal revenue obtained from selling an additional unit of output in any one market is the same for all the markets. (Robinson 1948, p. 181).

In other words, the optimal allocation criterion is to distribute marketing effort to segments so that the ratio of incremental revenue to incremental costs is the same for all segments. The important point here is that the theory of imperfect competition provides a basis for identifying the optimal aggregation and allocation criterion for a normative theory of market segmentation. Later, I will return to this distinction between aggregation and allocation criteria.

It was Wendell Smith who recognized the importance of these theories for marketing strategy. And that brings me to my third point, the development of demand criteria for segmentation strategies. Smith makes a statement that links market segmentation with the writings of Joan Robinson. He says "segmentation is disaggregative in its effects and tends to bring about recognition of several demand schedules where only one was recognized before." The recognition of several demand schedules produces two demand criteria in addition to response elasticity. First, segments can be defined by differences in utilities (that is, needs). This criterion defines what the demand curve is characterizing in the eyes of the consumer, namely a bundle of utilities that represents a brand.

Second, segments can be defined by the position of the demand curve, that is by the level of demand. And third, as noted, segments can be defined by response elasticity, that is, by the shape of the demand curve.

Since Wendell Smith's basic work, market segmentation has followed three broad approaches characterized by these three demand criteria. One approach has been clearly related to brand attribute utility. It has been referred to as benefit segmentation and is characterized by grouping consumers by similarity in the needs and/or brand attributes considered most important. The newer approaches involving conjoint analysis (Green and Wind 1975) and componential segmentation (Green 1977) clearly fall into this category.

The next two approaches can be generally referred to as behavioral as distinct from benefit segmentation (See Assael 1973). Segmenting by the position or the shape of the demand curve requires utilizing a behavioral rather than a perceptual criterion. (I would include purchase intent under behavioral segmentation even though it is a perceptual variable since it does define a predisposition to act).

Segmentation by the position of the demand curve relies on the criterion of quantity purchased. Reference to heavy versus light buyers or the "heavy half" is typical. Segmentation by brand purchased also is in this category despite the fact it is dichotomous since on the aggregate level, percent of consumers in a segment buying the brand is a reasonable proxy for volume. Typically, these criteria have been used as dependent variables with demographics, life-style or brand attitudes used as descriptor variables. Whereas benefit segmentation has been used primarily for new product development and positioning, segmenting by level of demand has been used to describe existing markets.

The third criterion, segmentation by response elasticities, is the only one that provides guidelines for resource allocation along the lines proposed by Joan Robinson. If elasticity can be determined on the individual level, then segments can be defined based on similarity in elasticities and resources allocated accordingly. Segmentation by price elasticity has its limits because of the obvious restrictions regarding price discrimination. But there could be direct applications to marketing strategy for deal, coupon or sales promotional elasticities all of which are related to price; and defining advertising elasticities would have direct implications for the level of marketing effort to each segment.

By the way, I have been referring to elasticity as the

optimal aggregation criterion and will soon be referring to a
study that challenges this view. Other bases for aggregating
consumers could be considered, such as marginal response, or
response function coefficients. But they all have one thing in
common; they require measurement of consumer responses to marketing stimuli on the individual level.

The three approaches to segmentation I just referred to,
their applications, and their degree of utilization are summarized in Table 1. As noted, the most important applications

TABLE 1

THREE DEMAND CRITERIA FOR MARKET SEGMENTATION

Demand Criteria	Applications	Amount of Past Use
1. Needs; Utilities (Benefit Segmentation)	New Product Development; Product Positioning	Heavy
2. Level of Demand (Behavioral Segmentation)	Description of Characteristics of target market; Selection of Components of marketing mix	Heavy
3. Response Elasticities (Behavioral Segmentation)	Level of marketing effort and allocation to market segments	Light to none

of benefit segmentation have been in the area of new product
development and utilization has been heavy. Segmentation by
level of demand has been used to develop and adjust the components of the marketing mix. The demographic, life-style or
attitudinal characteristics of heavy users, brand loyalists,
or regular brand users are identified and media, advertising
and distribution strategies are developed accordingly. Utilization here has also been heavy. Segmentation by response
elasticities has been applied to establishing the level of
marketing effort between segments. Utilization of this approach has been very light to non-existent.

The lack of utilization of response elasticity as a segmentation criterion is certainly not due to shortcomings in
terms of strategic relevance. It is due to the difficulty of
measuring elasticity. If the optimal aggregation and allocation criteria are to be utilized, elasticities must be measured
on the individual level. But how? Table 2 shows some methods.

TABLE 2

METHODS FOR MEASURING RESPONSE ELASTICITIES
ON THE INDIVIDUAL CONSUMER LEVEL

Method	Problem
1. Controlled store experiments	- Reliability of controls - Projectability - Small Sample for aggregation
2. Simulated in-store facilities	(Same as 1)
3. Self-report (e.g. Dollarmetrics)	- Validity of data - Reliability
4. Consumer panels	- No controls - Interpreting behavior

Controlled store experiments could be run in which consumer responses to changes in in-store conditions are tracked. Simulated in-store facilities could be used such as Yankelovich's LTM service or Elrick and Lavidge's COMP. But small-sample experiments may be insufficient to establish aggregation criteria for a number of segments that would then be generalizable to the total market. Paper and pencil tests could be used to assess the consumer's perceived sensitivity at various price levels. Woodside, Sharma and Bearden's Dollarmetric approach is an example (1979). But the validity and reliability of these perceptual measures is questionable.

Consumer panel data could also be utilized to attempt to establish elasticities on the individual level. But here, the problems are even more serious. There is no provision for controls to insure that response is due to changes in the marketing stimulus. Also, as Smith states, demand should be measured on a selective rather than on a primary basis, meaning that brand not product category elasticities should be measured. It then becomes difficult to assess whether a switch from one brand to another is a function of the marketing stimulus under study or some other variable. Variations in repurchase cycles add to the difficulty of measuring consumer response to marketing stimuli since the researcher cannot distinguish between a "no purchase" situation and a "normal" interval in the purchase sequence. Finally, variations in package size confound attempts to measure consumer responses to changes in marketing stimuli.

On the other side of the coin, the "new technology" may

assist researchers in measuring elasticities on the individual
level. Controlled experiments could be run in stores with
scanners. Panels of consumers who shop in such stores could be
tracked to determine changes in purchase behavior as a result
of changes in in-store conditions. As scanner data becomes
widespread, such experimentation could provide a more reliable
base for aggregation and allocation criteria. Split cable TV
could provide a more reliable basis for measuring advertising
elasticity. Matched samples of consumers could be tested with
different frequencies of exposure. As cable TV becomes more
widespread, such testing could also provide a more reliable
basis for marketing allocations.

The difficulty of utilizing elasticity criteria is demonstrated by the paucity of results in the literature. The few
attempts to segment by elasticity have predefined segments by
some other criterion and then determined elasticity on the aggregate level within the segment. Massy and Frank (1965) were
among the first to do so. Writing in 1965, they first state
the classical criterion of optimization, in this case regarding
advertising elasticities as follows:

> "The within group variances for the _individual_
> purchase promotional sensitivities should be small
> and the between group variance large."

Having stated that promotional elasticities should be measured
on the individual level, they then predefine segments by demographic criteria and measure elasticities within segments on an
aggregate basis.

There are two additional problems in utilizing criteria
of elasticity for purposes of segmentation. First, theoretically, maximization of profits is achieved if the marketer is
free to allocate resources to individual consumers. This of
course assumes there are no economies of scale in marketing, an
invalid assumption. But it must be recognized that in the
process of aggregation from the individual consumer level, some
point will be reached where further aggregation will reduce
profits. To my knowledge, only one study has come close to
establishing a criterion for defining the point where the decrease in marginal revenue from further aggregation is just
balanced by the reduction in marginal costs from economies of
scale. I will be citing this study shortly (Tollefson and
Lessig 1798).

Second, assuming segments have been defined by some criterion of elasticity, is the optimal allocation criterion reliable? Such a criterion would require comparing the marginal
revenues of segments to given levels of marketing stimuli.

14

Presumably, if segments can be defined by elasticity criteria, then their marginal responses and marginal revenues can be determined. But are the underlying causes of marginal revenues comparable across segments? Can one be assured that responses in all segments are equally a function of sensitivity to the marketing stimulus under consideration? Assume that a given segment has a higher ratio of marginal revenue to marginal advertising expenditure than other segments. Is it not possible this segment is reacting to other conditions (e.g. greater sensitivity to word-of-mouth information)?

Let me add one other wrinkle to the problems of utilizing individual elasticities as an optimal criterion for segmentation. I mentioned the need for establishing an aggregation and an allocation criterion. Recent doubt has been expressed whether elasticity is in fact the optimal criterion for defining segments. I am referring to an article in the August 1978 issue of the Journal of Marketing Research (the special market segmentation issue) by Tollefson and Lessig (1978). Tollefson and Lessig suggest that the optimal criterion for segmentation is to combine aggregation and allocation into one criterion for profit maximization. As noted, the theoretical ideal for allocation is to treat each consumer as a separate segment and allocate according to their marginal response, assuming no economies of scale. Tollefson and Lessig state the optimal aggregation criterion is to combine two segments so that the consequent profit reduction is minimized. Further, they suggest that the aggregation criterion is contingent on the allocation criterion since their optimal aggregation criterion requires defining individual consumer reactions to various sets of marketing variables. This proposal appears logical and is theoretically superior to traditional views that separate the aggregation and allocation criteria and define optimal aggregation based on similarity of elasticities. But if there are problems in operationalizing the criterion of elasticity on the individual level, consider the problems in operationalizing Tollefson and Lessig's optimal criterion. To operationalize their segmentation criterion requires one to know how each segment or individual will respond to various levels of marketing activity. Implementation requires knowing not only optimal response and allocation levels, but also near optimal levels, and then estimating the profit consequences of aggregating two or more consumers. Such complete knowledge of one's market is rarely if ever available. Thus, although theoretically sound, the information requirements of the Tollefson and Lessig criterion make its implementation impractical.

I started out by defining segmentation by elasticities on the individual level as the optimal segmentation criterion. I

15

expressed serious reservations about the practicality of such an approach. I then cited a challenge to this traditional view and a definition of an optimal criterion based on minimization in profit loss in the process of aggregation, but expressed even more serious reservations about the feasibility of such an approach. Where does all this leave us? Where do we go from here? Table 3 provides a perspective on future applications.

TABLE 3

FUTURE ADVANCES IN MARKET SEGMENTATION

Method	Future Applications
Benefit Segmentation	Componential segmentation
Segmentation by level of demand	Segment Congruence Analysis

Segmentation by response elasticities	1. Improvements in measurement
	  - Scanner Data
	  - Cable TV
	2. Improvements in aggregation criteria
	  - marginal response or
	  - response coefficients or
	  - elasticities

It seems that we have a handle on benefit segmentation. Traditional approaches to defining homogeneous groups based on similarity in needs will continue to be relevant. Further, methodologies for concept formulation and testing through conjoint analysis will be strengthened with the application of componential segmentation techniques (Green 1977). These techniques seek to combine product features and consumer characteristics in the analysis of attribute utilities. An orthogonal array of consumer types and product features is developed, and a product by consumer matrix is submitted for analysis. Predictions can then be made of the optimal product characteristics for any combination of consumer characteristics.

We also have a handle on segmenting by level of demand. Again traditional approaches defining the characteristics of behavioral segments by life styles, attitudes, demographics and needs will continue. The primary focus here will also continue to be on methodological issues, for example, the

16

treatment of multiple dependent variables or the introduction
of interactive variables for behavioral predictions. But more
work is likely to be needed on comparing the bases for segmentation. Here, segment congruence analysis (Green and
Carmone 1977) holds some promise as a means of comparing
classes of descriptor variables so as to guide the researcher
to the most powerful descriptor set.

We have gone a long way regarding benefit segmentation
and segmenting by level of demand since Wendell Smith's original article. But we have not gone very far in utilizing
normative criteria for segmentation. Yet it seems these are
the criteria that Smith was emphasizing because he continuously
refers to the problems of marketing resource allocation in the
context of market segmentation. I believe more work will be
done in analyzing consumer response functions to marketing
stimuli, particularly the very important issue that Tollefson
and Lessig raised, the nature of the optimal aggregation criterion. In some sense, it may be too early in the state of
the art of market segmentation to raise the issue whether
aggregation should be by elasticity, marginal response, or response function coefficients. We have to overcome the problem
of data collection so that consumer responses can be linked to
marketing stimuli over time. Therefore, it is likely that more
refined attempts at experimentation utilizing simulated environments, scanner stores and cable TV, will be attempted in
the future.

This leaves us with an important challenge, to attempt to
operationalize normative criteria of segmentation so that
twenty-five years from now, when Wendell Smith and I are back
together in this forum, we can cite further advances in the
applications of normative segmentation criteria.

REFERENCES

Assael, Henry (1973), "Segmenting Market Segmentation Strategies and Techniques," European Research, 1 (September), 190-
194; and 1 (November), 256-258.

_____ and A. Marvin Roscoe, Jr. (1976), "Approaches to
Market Segmentation Analysis," Journal of Marketing, 40
(October), 67-76.

Chamberlin, E. H. (1946), Theory of Monopolistic Competition,
Harvard University Press, Cambridge, Mass.

Claycamp, Henry J. and William F. Massy (1968), "A Theory of
Market Segmentation," Journal of Marketing Research, 5

(November), 388-394.

Frank, Ronald E., William F. Massy and Yoram Wind (1972), Market Segmentation, Prentice-Hall, Inc.: Englewood Cliffs, New Jersey.

Green, Paul E. (1977), "A New Approach to Market Segmentation," Business Horizons, 20 (February), 61-73.

_____ and Frank J. Carmone (1977), "Segment Congruence Analysis: A Method for Analyzing Association Among Alternative Bases for Market Segmentation," Journal of Consumer Research 3 (March), pp. 217-222.

_____ and Yoram Wind (1975), "New Ways to Measure Consumers' Judgments," Harvard Business Review, 53 (July-August), 107-117.

Massy, William F. and Ronald E. Frank (1965), "Short Term Price and Dealing Effects in Selected Market Segments," Journal of Marketing Research, 2 (May), 171-185.

Robinson, Joan (1948), The Economics of Imperfect Competition, MacMillan and Co., London.

Smith, Wendell R. (1956), "Product Differentiation and Market Segmentation as Alternative Marketing Strategies," Journal of Marketing, 21 (July), 3-8.

Tollefson, John O. and Parker Lessig (1978), "Aggregation Criteria in Normative Market Segmentation Theory," Journal of Marketing Research, 15 (August), 346-355.

Wind, Yoram (1978), "Issues and Advances in Segmentation Research," Journal of Marketing Research, 15 (August), 317-337.

Woodwide, Arch, Alok K. Sharma and William O. Bearden (1979), "A Dollarmetric Approach for Estimating Consumer Brand Loyalty," Presentation at the American Marketing Association's 10th Attitude Research Conference.

MARKET SEGMENTATION: A REVIEW OF ITS PROBLEMS AND PROMISE

Frederick W. Winter, University of Illinois, Champaign-Urbana

Few concepts have become of more importance to virtually all marketers than the concept of market segmentation.

This paper will briefly trace the development of the concept starting with its conceptualization by Smith in 1956 (Smith 1956) and ending with some recent findings.

Market segmentation is a concept used by practitioners, academic researchers and strategists. Below are two job-related classified advertisements from the Wall Street Journal.

> ...step up to a diversified consumer product marketing-manager...We require one disciplined in product (market evaluation techniques, market segmentation, the optimum marketing mix, marketing plan development), costs, and communications...

> Our company is a market leader in...transportation equipment...This position is responsible for the analysis of target markets, product management, strategy development, and special investment projects.

Indeed, whether called market segmentation or target marketing, the concept is widely recognized as an important analysis technique in the practitioner's way of doing business.

In a widely quoted article on the Product Matrix Strategy of the Boston Consulting Group, Cox (Cox 1974, pg. 465-470) cites a method to "achieve and maintain market dominance."

> Market segmentation - this is the key to the successful application of product portfolio strategy, for it provides the means of changing the category of any entry in the Growth-Share Matrix. Selection of the most appropriate market segments is directed by the matrix parameters of dominant share opportunity and high growth rates, but limited by a lack of models for optimizing segment selection.

It seems obvious that by segmenting a market we change the definition of the market, and therefore alter the market share and the growth potential of the market. In fact, we also affect market share because segmenting often leads to different competitors:

> Data suggests that certain kinds of whiskey may compete more closely with brandy than they do with other kinds of whiskey. (Stefflre 1968)

Academic researchers, too, devoted substantial efforts to segmentation. Segmentation has spawned three books (Engel 1972; Frank 1972; and Scotton 1980), and an issue of the Journal of Marketing Research (1978) was devoted to this topic. Countless seminars and conferences have been held that attest to the interest in the topic.

The Beginning

The concept of market segmentation originated with economists who referred to price discrimination. True amplification of the principle, however, came from Smith 25 years ago, who provided the following definition:

> ...Segmentation is based upon developments of the demand side of the market and represents a rational and more precise adjustment of product and marketing effort to consumer or user requirements. In the language of the economist, segmentation is disaggregative in its effects and tends to bring about recognition of several demand schedules where only one was recognized before...

> ...Market segmentation, on the other hand, consists of viewing a heterogeneous market (one characterized by divergent demand) as a number of smaller homogeneneous markets in response to differing product preferences among important market segments. It is attributable to the desires of consumers or users for more precise satisfaction of their varying wants...

Smith contrasted segmentation with product differentiation, which he referred to as a promotion strategy:

> In its simplest terms, product differentiation is securing a measure of control over the demand for a product by advertising or promoting differences between a product and the products of competing sellers. It is basically the result of sellers' desires to establish firm market positions and/or to insulate their businesses against price competition. Differentiation tends to be

20

characterized by heavy use of advertising and
promotion and to result in prices that are
somewhat above the equilibrium levels associated
with perfectly competitive market conditions.
It may be classified as a <u>promotional</u> strategy
or approach to marketing.

Today these two concepts are considered similar; nevertheless,
at the time Smith's message had important impact on marketers
who were anxious to break out of pricing-based models of
consumer behavior. Furthermore, the paper was an initial
attempt to extend the definition of the marketing mix.

15 Years of Regression

The phase following Smith's introduction can best be
described as the Dark Ages of Market Segmentation. Indeed,
it was "15 years of regression" for several reasons. First,
the standard segmentation method was to measure how much product was consumed and then relate this variable to demographic
variables via multiple regression analysis. Secondly, it was
regression because it was a giant step backward from Smith's
original contribution.

It is easy to take Smith's phrase divergent demand and
jump to Frank's (1972) statement:

1. To what extent should a firm pursue a
   strategy of market segmentation?

   ...It is normal to answer the first
   question in the affirmative if it
   can be shown that, on the average,
   certain segments (groups) of people
   buy more of the product under consideration than do other groups...

   ...We have found it useful to think
   of these criteria in terms of the
   following question:

2. What is the degree of variation in
   the average level of customer demand
   for the product from one segment to
   another? ...

Smith, if we read carefully, referred to divergent demand
<u>schedules</u> not divergent demand <u>levels</u>. A demand schedule is
a quantity response to elements of the marketing mix; a demand
level is quantity demanded at a particular level of the

21

marketing mix. To set the record straight, Frank did mention elements of response as a criterion for segmentation:

3. What is the degree of variation in customer sensitivity to changes in the firm's promotional policies as well as those of competitors?

Heavy Half Explored

By doing some minor algebraic manipulations, it is possible to see the implications of marketing to the "heavy half" and how this relates to demand response. Total demand for brand j is simply the sum of demands for brand j by the n individuals in the market:

$$D_j = \sum_{i=1}^{n} d_{ij} \qquad (1)$$

Demand by an individual, d_{ij}, is a function of the individual's demand for the product class d_i, as well as his market share awarded to brand j, ms_{ij}. Therefore,

$$D_j = \sum_{i=1}^{n} d_i \cdot ms_{ij} \qquad (2)$$

If we differentiate D_j with respect to a marketing mix variable m (i.e., price, promotion, a product feature, etc.) we get

$$\frac{dD_j}{dm} = \sum_{i=1}^{n} d_i \cdot \frac{dMS_{ij}}{dm} + MS_{ij} \frac{dd_i}{dm} \cdot \qquad (3)$$

In other words, the greatest demand response will result when the marketer is able to:

1) increase demand for the product class among those for whom your brand would get a high market share.

or,

2) increase his market share to heavy users.

It was Honda that successfully implemented the first strategy by ignoring the Harley Davidson heavy users and targeted for the nonusers to whom "you meet the nicest people on a Honda" would guarantee a high market share.

22

There is no strong empirical evidence in the literature to indicate that heavy users are particularly sensitive to marketing mix manipulations and therefore a particularly rewarding target. Furthermore, the work of Tollefson and Lessig (1978) indicate that the heavy user is not a good surrogate for the essence of the segmentation objective.

Over-Reliance on Demographics and Identification Issues

The marketing community seems not only obsessed with its fascination for the heavy user but it couples this with its need to identify this person using demographic variables.

As Wind (1978) says in his excellent summary of the state of segmentation, the choice of variables should be based on the "actionability" of the variables. Demographics are not particularly actionable. If we get a demographic profile of our target, it gives us some media candidates. Nevertheless, critique of this approach has shown that omitted variables can lead to incorrect decisions. Perhaps the most dramatic demonstration has to do with an example this author has discovered when using demographics for geographic distribution. It turns out that the demographic profile of a heavy user of X rated movies has a pretty good match with the profile of Salt Lake City, Utah. This has obviously ignored what we know about the religious character of that particular city.

Therefore, demographics should only be used to screen a large list of candidates (e.g., media, geographic locations, etc.) to a smaller list (Winter 1980). After that, it becomes necessary to do some direct analysis (e.g., segment membership versus media readership, site surveys, etc.). This will tend to minimize the "omitted variable" problem.

There also seems to be the mentality that if segments are not identifiable, the market is not segmentable. Kotler (1980), in his classic text, refers to the need for "accessibility" as a criteria for "effective segmentation." Green (1977), in discussing componential segmentation--a method to see if consumer characteristics are related to response to product features, says:

> ...a useful measure is computed that shows how "segmentable" the market is, with respect to the stimuli and background variables used in the study. The segmentability index is simply a measure of how large the interaction sum of squares (persons x stimuli) is, relative to the total variation in the data. In the present problem, the effect of the interaction term was quite

23

small (about 8% of the total), suggesting that
this market was not highly segmentable.

What is often ignored is the strategy of self-selection first
described by Frank, Massy and Wind (1972). If the market for
particular benefits is there, even though they cannot be identified, it may be useful to segment the market. Although promotion cannot be targeted, it may still be worthwhile to produce the product features, at a price, using the distribution
favored by a particular segment. Instead of a rifle promotion
approach, we will probably have to use a shotgun approach--
resulting in higher costs that could, very easily, be offset
by higher revenues.

One potentially important use of demographics is in the
industrial marketing context. Generally, industrial marketers
have fewer options available when compared with their consumer
marketing counterparts. The potential for using demographic
identification is enhanced because:

1. Sales is the primary promotional technique, and
   thus the contact is one-on-one, and

2. The demographic characteristics (e.g., SIC code,
   etc.) of the potential purchasers are known prior
   to the sales call.

Thus, our ability to identify segments could have importance
in developing call norms, allocating a salesforce, developing
salesforce quotas, and other critical decisions.

Normative Segmentation

If segmentation models were to be classified, one relevant
classification would be descriptive models and normative models.
Descriptive models have been discussed but normative models of
segmentation have undergone substantial change. The classic
piece in normative segmentation is often considered to be by
Claycamp and Massy (1968). Claycamp and Massy consider segmentation to be an aggregative process. Ideally, we would
segment at the individual level, but a series of constraints
in terms of legal restrictions, data availability and use of
common media force us to assume a higher and higher level of
aggregation. The authors refer to the ideal form of segmentation:

The theory shows that optimal profits can be
achieved if the firm uses consumers' marginal
responses to price, i.e., price elasticities, to
define mutually exclusive segments ....

24

It took ten years for this aggregation on the basis of response or elasticities to be challenged by Tollefson and Lessig (1978), who simulated consumer data and showed that aggregation on the basis of either response or elasticities are not ideal strategies. The heuristic that comes closest to ideal is: group two segments together if the two segments require similar optimal levels to the marketing mix. Although the reason for the failure of aggregating on the basis of response on elasticities is not clearly stated, it most likely appears to be that both are revenue oriented--they ignore the cost side of the equation. Using two alternative demand schedules, the two bases for grouping response coefficients and elasticities do not fare well.

The Tollefson and Lessig ideal method of segmentation is one where we minimize loss by combining the two subsegments together. According to the authors, this results in the minimum loss. Thus, they explicitly state that profit will be largest when a totally disaggregative approach is taken. It seems unrealistic, however, that n marketing mixes will not be more expensive than n-1. In fact, there is a fixed cost associated any time a new marketing mix (which may include a new distribution alternative or new media used is offered). The notion of limited resources has been advanced by Mahajan and Jain (1978), and Winter (1979) has modelled the impact of fixed costs on mix selection. These two articles in particular offer practical as well as theoretically rich approaches to market segmentation.

Accordingly, a new definition of market segmentation that is compatible with recent advances in theory and practice is:

> Market segmentation is the recognition that
> groups or subsegments differ with respect to pro-
> perties which suggest that different marketing
> mixes might be used to appeal to the different
> groups. We then may aggregate these subsegments
> to reduce costs more than benefits (revenues)
> and the aggregation is based on the fact that
> they both respond most to the same marketing mix.

As shown in Figure 1, the number of marketing mixes offered will affect both costs and revenues. If few subsegments are aggregated (many marketing mixes), revenue will have reached asymptotic levels, but costs will be very high. This shows the need for cost-benefit considerations. Table 1, adapted from Winter (1979), shows that aggregation on the basis of appeal of similar marketing mixes can lead to aggregation of rather dissimilar subsegments; note that marketing mix 8 is offered to both subsequents 3 and 4.

FIGURE 1

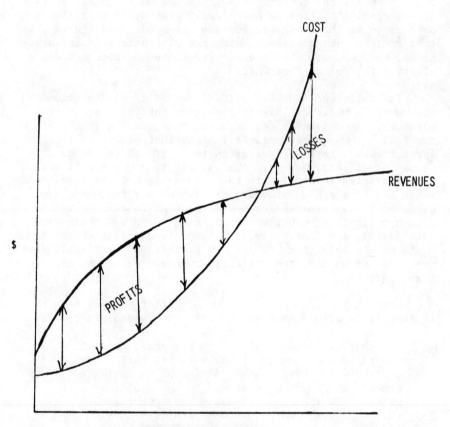

NUMBER OF MARKETING MIXES

TABLE 1

TABLE 1
Segment-Marketing Mix Profit Matrix for Gasohol Market

Aggregate Market

Market Subsegments

| Mix No. | Mix Definition | | | | | | | | | Fixed Cost FC (000) |
	D^1	P^2	L^3	A^4	O^5	I	II	III	IV	
1	S	70	L	5	89	592.4[6]	0	57.2	0	30
2	S	70	U	10	93	197.5	36.8	19.0	0	30
3	S	76	U	5	93	.3	147.0	76.2	0	30
4	S	76	U	10	93	30.1	165.4	85.8	0	30
5	UC	70	L	5	93	209.6	0	38.4	72.0	50
6	UC	70	L	10	93	262.1	0	48.0	90.0	50
7	UC	76	L	5	89	0	0	0	234.0	50
8	UC	76	L	10	93	42.5	0	105.2	216.0	50
9	UN	70	L	10	89	713.9	0	0	0	160

[1] Distribution: S=Standard, UC=unbranded stations accepting credit cards, UN=unbranded
stations not accepting credit cards
[2] Price: 70=70c/gallon, 76=76c/gallon
[3] Leaded/Unleaded: L=leaded, U=unleaded
[4] Alcohol Content: 5=5% alcohol content, 10=10% alcohol content
[5] Octane Rating
[6] Figures in matrix represent gross profit before fixed costs, ᴛ (000 omitted).

From: Winter (1979)

Operational Definitions

When groups are formed in segmentation analysis, the critical criterion always becomes "how does the ideal marketing mix that you would use for this group differ from that which you would use on other groups?" This immediately indicates why media exposure data is much more sensible to use than a surrogate collection of measures like demographics.

Less trivial examples become rather complicated although technology is catching up. For example, some results using conjoint analysis seem to indicate that response to product characteristics can be measured. How, for example, do we measure response for advertising?

The standard solution is to use surrogate measures--such as communication based measures: "If a person hasn't heard of the product they will probably be more responsive to mass media advertising than a person who has already tried the product". There have been some attempts to relate response to demographic characteristics--these were useful. It would now be useful to relate response to information that could be easily elicited from the respondent. For example, if an instrument were

27

developed that was a valid measure of response to advertising or price sensitivity, managers could better use marketing research to develop segmentation plans. The attempt to link demographics to response was in the right spirit but imposed the additional requirement that response is, in fact, related to demographics. It would appear that product/situation-specific measures might hold more promise.

SUMMARY

The future of market segmentation as an aid to the practice of marketing, indeed looks bright. After a period of false starts, a body of literature is beginning to emerge that helps us to understand the true implications.

To a great extent, Wendell Smith should share both in the credit for its beginning, the blame for its false start, and the credit for the future. Professor Smith provided a conceptual base in 1956 that is still relevant today. If researchers and practitioners had carefully followed his concept, the period of the "Dark Ages of Segmentation" would not have resulted. It was unfortunate that he assumed administrative duties and did not remain active in the area. Regarding his contribution, I might quote what a tennis coach once said about my tennis stroke, "A great start but no follow through." But oh what a start he gave us!

REFERENCES

Claycamp, Henry J. and William F. Massy (1968), "A Theory of Market Segmentation," Journal of Marketing Research, 5 (November), pp. 388-394.

Cox, William E., Jr. (1974), "Product Portfolio Strategy: A Review of the Boston Consulting Group Approach to Marketing Strategy," 1974 Combined Proceedings of the American Marketing Association, 36, pp. 465-470.

Engel, James F., Henry F. Fiorillo and Murray A. Cayley (1972), Market Segmentation, Holt, Rinehart, and Winston, New York.

Frank, Ronald E. (1968), "Market Segmentation Research: Findings and Implications," in Frank M. Bass, Charles W. King and Edgar A. Pessemier, eds., The Application of the Sciences to Marketing Management, Wiley, New York, pp. 39-68.

_____, William Massy and Yoram Wind (1972), Market Segmentation, Prentice Hall, Engelwood Cliffs.

Green, Paul E. (1977), "A New Approach to Market Segmentation," Business Horizons, (February), pp. 61-73.

Kotler, Philip D. (1980), Marketing Management: Analysis Planning and Control, Prentice Hall, Engelwood Cliffs, pp. 205-206.

Journal of Marketing Research (1978), American Marketing Association, 15 (August).

Mahajan, Vijay and Arun K. Jain (1978), "An Approach to Normative Segmentation," Journal of Marketing Research, 15 (August), pp. 338-345.

Scotton, Donald W. and Ronald L. Zallocco (1980), Readings in Market Segmentation, American Marketing Association, Chicago.

Smith, Wendell (1956), "Product Differentiation and Market Segmentation as Alternative Marketing Strategies," Journal of Marketing, 21, (July), pp. 3-8.

Stefflre, Volney (1968), "Market Structure Studies: New Products for Old Markets and New Markets (Foreign) for Old Products," in Frank M. Bass, Charles W. King and Edgar A. Pessemier, eds., The Application of the Science to Marketing Management, Wiley, New York, pp. 251-268.

Tollefson, John O. and V. Parker Lessig (1978), "Aggregative Criteria in Normative Segmentation Theory," Journal of Marketing Research, 15 (August), pp. 346-355.

Wind, Yoram (1978), "Issues and Advances in Segmentation Research," Journal of Marketing Research, 15 (August), pp. 317-337.

Winter, Frederick W. (1979), "A Cost-Benefit Approach to Market Segmentation," Journal of Marketing, 43 (Fall), pp. 103-11.

Winter, Frederick W. (1980), "Match Target Markets to Media Audiences," Journal of Advertising Research, 20 (February), pp. 61-65.

THE PHYSICS AND THE METAPHYSICS OF MARKETING

Robert Bartels, Ohio State University

Periodically the marketing faculty have assembled in special conference to share breakthroughs in the conceptual reference in which marketing is beheld. In 1914, reputedly the first scientific presentation of the subject of marketing was made by L. D. H. Weld before the American Economic Association. In 1946, a small group of marketing professors met in Pittsburgh for a first discussion of the scientific character of the marketing discipline. In 1957, a few scholars with international interests met in Boston to establish a conceptual structure for comparative marketing analysis. In the 1960s, the Marketing Theory Seminar participants meeting in Colorado and Vermont explored new ramifications of the marketing theory. In 1976, the first Macromarketing conference was held in Boulder. It is reasonable to think that the conferees of the Paul D. Converse Awards could also yield further insights to enrich the development of marketing thought. Toward this end, I wish to share some thoughts concerning the opportunity we have, through marketing, to contribute to the betterment of mankind.

Economic and social development throughout the world awaits the conception of new ideas, and it is a responsibility of marketing scholars to answer whether they have a contribution to make. Society has not generally looked to marketing for the solution of some of its problems. Instead, it has often regarded marketing as the cause of them: the exploitation of markets, the disruption of life styles, the waste of resources. Unfortunately, much of the world has not experienced the best that marketing has to offer, for marketing technology has been least applied in underdeveloped areas, where need for it is greatest. Yet many within the marketing profession have conviction that marketing can more widely meet basic consumption needs and yield additional benefits of larger nature.

While marketing thought broadly encompasses the laws of physical distribution, it is still ethnocentric, built around a core of American experience, and provincial, assuming that what has been successful here is applicable elsewhere. This characteristic notwithstanding, marketing has long been attributed universality, because trade occurs everywhere. Even conceptually, universality has been attributed to it, for when originally classified, the marketing functions, which initially comprised "marketing," were said to be "inherent, pervasive, and _universal_." The concept of universality gained further credence when, within the universe of our own society, the laws or principles of marketing were seen to have consistency throughout time and in different lines of trade.

Whether or not marketing _practice_ be universal, the same cannot be confidently said of marketing _theory_, if by universality is meant worldwide applicability. The discipline has not been based upon multinational evidence nor meant to be applied globally. It evolved as a body of thought for marketing practice in a developed, industrialized economy. In the eyes of many other nations, it is associated with a culture that is capitalistic, affluent, and materialistic. It is not seen to be a factor _contributing_ to economic development, and underdeveloped economies, excluded by this image of marketing from its "universality," are content to let production develop before considering marketing. Consequently, marketing theory, macro or micro, has had little place in development plans. If marketing scholars and theorists are content with such an image of marketing, we may never carry the mission of marketing to needy countries, and they may be left to rediscover marketing in their own domestic circumstances. But this need not be.

The problem is that our field of study has been too narrow to provide the generalizations required for meeting global needs. The remedy lies in studying not merely _marketing_ around the world, but rather the _diversity_ of marketing. The reasons for differences must be understood if cross-cultural transfers are to be made. Within the context of our own society, our theories present alternative courses of action appropriate under our different circumstances, but people of foreign cultures see them not as _options_ applicable to their situations, but as _prescriptions_ which appear to them to be sometimes inapplicable. A marketing principle states a relationship that, given Cause A, Consequence B will tend to follow. If market situation A prevails, marketing action B will be appropriate. In contrasting societies, situations A may be opposite in character, so that actions B will differ in two countries. Unless this is explicitly indicated by marketing principles which make evident the appropriateness of _both_, or opposite actions, little counsel can be given outside one's own realm. Marketing principles have been stated too onesidedly; in global perspective the entire range of A : B relationships would be implied. Thus principles would have universality in that they would be everywhere applicable and valid.

Three principles may be cited which are derivable from global analysis but which would not be evident in the study of

31

a single country:

1. It is observed that marketing practices which are
successful in one country may fail in another, because their
circumstances differ. With technology transfer, however,
practices tend to become alike. This is sometimes decried as
the "Americanization" of a developing country, and the technology exporter may believe that what was right in the United
States is right for anywhere. The fact is that "right" is
relative, and convergence of practice is possible only because
of growing similarity of circumstances. Domestically-derived
principles may not reveal this, unless the generalization were
inferred from evolution through time rather than through space.
Yet without this intelligence one could not fully understand or
contribute to economic development through marketing. A
Principle of Convergence might be stated as follows: that with
industrialization of a country, employment of marketing practices of another industrialized country is not emulation, but
rather adoption of that which is indigenous to all industrial-
ized countries. Such a principle is thought to have universality.

2. With progressive industrialization, the expectations
of marketing held by society also change. A. H. Maslow identified a hierarchy of five levels of employee job-satisfaction
expectations. A similar progression is shown by global study
to characterize the expectations of nations. Maslow's categories identified need progressively for sustenance and survival,
safety and security, satisfaction in human interaction, external
approval, and finally internal satisfaction and self-fulfillment.
Nations similarly first expect marketing to supply basic consumption needs, then better management skills, fuller customer
satisfaction, and ultimately social responsibility. The pattern
is pervasive and universal, and it suggests a Principle of Expectation, namely, that the expectation of marketing varies
directly with the advancement of social and economic development.

3. A corollary of the Principle of Expectation is that
compliance with expectations varies directly with the capability
of marketers or the economy profitably to fulfill them.

There are many such universals to be found in multiple-
society analysis. "Marketing" itself is found to be a subset
of the generic process of society's meeting its consumption
needs in a manner indigenous to its development and culture,
by whatever name the process may be called. Mass distribution
is seen of necessity to coincide with and depend upon mass
production, if that production is for the local market and not
for export. The full-function wholesalers' dominance of distribution channels is seen generally to diminish with the industrialization of an economy. Retail price haggling decreases, and

consumerism increases with industrialization.

Such propositions may seem simple, even self-evident, possibly capable of being inferred from the study of one society through time, but until they are verbalized they have no fixity in marketing thought, and until they are derived from global analysis they are inferred and not demonstrated. Validly universal marketing principles alone are a sound basis for macro and micro marketing administration.

The globalization of marketing adds a dimension to theory which is significant to academics and practitioners alike. The academic sees the coincidence of time and place factors in the evolution of marketing patterns; sees the wave-like movements of causal factors progressing throughout the world under different political regimes and cultural heritages; sees the locus of comparative makreting advantage shifting from region to region; and sees beforehand the course of marketing development yet to occur. The marketing practitioner or counselor sees that the scope of practice is confined to the limits imposed by one's concept of marketing; sees the contribution which marketing may make to economic development when its technology is scientifically adapted to prevailing local circumstances; and sees the adaptability of universal principles to a variety of circumstances.

Perception of marketing in global context is sufficiently different from domestic, international, and comparative concepts of marketing to afford a new basis for solving some of the marketing problems of the world and for contributing to economic development. It helps to answer the question of whether the marketing profession has a contribution to make to the betterment of mankind. Yet exclusive preoccupation with the physics of marketing, with "knowledge treating of the material world and its phenomena," as physics is defined in the dictionary, is not the only source of inspiration for conceptual breakthroughs for the improvement of marketing and the better meeting of human consumption needs.

It is recognized that marketing theory and practice have changed with changing concepts of marketing. It is equally true, although perhaps less recognized, that similar developments have occurred in response to changing concepts of man. We have seen the effects upon theory and practice of the change from regarding man as an "economic man" to a concept of him as a "whole society entity." As we have acknowledged man's "rights" as divinely bestowed upon him, his equality not to be discriminated against, his inherent integrity not to be defiled by deception, his dominion not to be subordinated by the State-- as these concepts of man have become accepted in our social and

professional thinking, they have been incorporated into marketing theories, laws, ethics, and policies.

These perceptions commit the marketer to a service con-
ditioned by factors outside the realm of physical marketing and
related to "the science of being, and...the science of the
fundamental causes and processes in things," phrases which
define metaphysics. Scientists and philosophers have sought to
understand and verbalize the "fundamental" determinants of human
experience. A provocative proposition has been advanced by a
distinguished Canadian mathematical physicist and biologist, Dr.
Glen W. Schaefer, who has said that "some scientists are begin-
ing to suggest that what we perceive is determined by what we
deeply believe," that the assumptions of the human mind determine our universe, and that our theories and our lives are the
detailed unfoldment of those assumptions. A change of assumptions changes the universe as we see it and sets one to act
from a different standpoint.

This suggests that, consciously or not, mankind has built
a process of supply and distribution upon certain assumptions:
that man's existence and survival are dependent upon material
consumption, and that consumable supplies must first be produced
and then distributed by the process called marketing. As marketers, in theory and in practice we have undertaken to close
the gap between producers and consumers and thus to render a
commendable service in facilitating consumption. An effort to
globalize the concept of this work is consistent with these
assumptions, but it is a physical rather than a metaphysical
way of regarding the activity. A metaphysician would assume
that above (meta) the conception of man as material and
materially dependent is a higher conception of him as spiritual,
of his need (including human need) being met by spiritual means,
and of the marketing process being the counterpart or the high-
est visible human expression of the spiritual fact.

Serious consideration of the question of spiritual determination and of a metaphysical concept of man, which have long
held the attention of thinkers, compels the marketer to philo-
sophize concerning life rather than just marketing, and to find
a spiritual modus operandi consistent with his professional
motivation to be a benefactor of human needs. The application
of a metaphysical perspective is found in historic accounts of
men to whom spiritual causation was a natural determinant of
human experience. More than once, for himself and for hundreds
of others, material consumption needs were supplied by spiritual
means by that master metaphysician, Jesus. Anterior to his time,
by assumptions refuting that conventional processes of production and marketing are required, other metaphysicians--
Elijah, Elisha, Moses, Joseph, and others--similary met

consumption needs, materializing products which had not been conventionally produced, presenting them where needed, and prolonging the supply of provisions.

The full potential of which the metaphysician is capable, to achieve the attainment of human consumption needs without conventional processes of production and distribution will not be realized so long as materialistic concepts of man persist, for as Schaefer indicates, our theories and our lives are the detailed unfoldment of our assumptions. Marketing changes for the better, however, has already occurred as we have improved our regard for man, and these changes foretell the lines along which further progress will be made. Marketing may be expected to become more satisfying, communication more informative, life-style values more substantial, transactions more honest, and the processes of distribution more reliable. Incorporated into daily experience, these are some of the offerings by which marketers can bring betterment to mankind.

The extent to which one takes a metaphysical approach to marketing may depend upon whether he approaches the subject as marketer or as man. Professionalism has led to acting in the capacity of the former, and our theories have been those of the physics of marketing, rather than those based upon the concept of determinants and processes "above," as implied by meta. Marketing theory has been unilinear along physical lines, but a redirection of thought may be achieved if emphasis is placed upon the meeting of human needs, rather than upon the distribution of products. As higher capabilities mature, we will do well to bring our theories of the physics of marketing to a broader base of generalization by seeking its universal verities, independent of time, space, and other differentiating circumstances. The mission of marketers is global, and the answer to whether we have a contribution to make to the betterment of the world is, unquestionably, "Yes!"

ON A METATHEORY OF SOCIAL BEHAVIOR

James M. Carman, University of California, Berkeley

I suspect we could agree that there has been no scholar in marketing who has done as much to create interest in the development of the nature of theory in marketing as Bob Bartels. A legion of graduate students have learned most of what they know about the development of marketing thought by reading Bartels' works. It is because of this that he has had the dubious distinction of making such a major contribution to the field as to be elected to receive this Paul D. Converse award for outstanding contributions to the theory of marketing and at the same time to be the perpetrator of one of the greatest myths currently established in our discipline. The myth is that "the study of marketing began early in the 20th century" (Bartels, 1970, p. v, italics in the original). The more complete Bartels' quote tells us,

> The first period of theory and metatheory development was one of pretheory theorization. It began with the initial study of marketing as a new subject, soon after the beginning of the 20th century, and it extended into the 1920s. It was a stage of thought development in which neither a definable theory was achieved nor a metatheory considered; yet theorization, or theoretical speculation, progressed along several lines. This was a stage in which the field of inquiry became identified, conceptualized, defined, and classified. (Ibid., pp. 16-17).

Marketing students who go beyond that first formal course segment on the development of thought now realize, of course, that this first period of pretheory theorization is as old as pretheories of economic activity. Aristotle, Plato, St. Augustine, and St. Thomas Acquinas all developed systematic pretheories of marketing. (See Dixon, 1979, 1980). There was enough systematic work on marketing done between the twelfth and fourteenth centuries that scholars actually cited one another (Nider, 1966). In seventeeth-century England, one hundred years before Adam Smith but after the reformation, the mercantilists had developed scholarly writing on marketing that were no longer tied to monastic scholarship. The word "merchandising" was defined in the seventeenth century in the same way it was in the U.S. in the early twentieth century (Wheeler, 1601; Barbon, 1690).

When preparing this paper, I thought for a short while
that this "Bartels' fallacy" may have come from Paul D. Converse
himself, for in Chapter 2 of the book we honor, Bartels cites
the 1959 Converse monograph, The Beginning of Marketing Thought
in the United States (Bartels, 1970, p. 17). However, this
certainly is not the case. For one thing, Converse clearly
restricts himself to the U.S. literature. For another,
Bartels' ideas on the history of marketing thought were formu-
lated in his dissertation, completed in 1941. I suspect the
fault lies in the research design for that dissertation.
Bartels relied largely on the oral histories and writings of
early U.S. marketing scholars, many of whom were still alive.
These roots led in large part from the Wisconson institutional
economists, W. H. Scott, John R. Commons, Richard T. Ely, and
H. C. Taylor. This group of progressive economists were not
ignorant of economic history in England and were probably
acquainted with the classical Latin scholars' views on economics and marketing. Alfred Marshall's Principles of Economics appeared in 1890 and quickly became the "culminating
achievement of neo-classical equilibrium economists" (John
Commons' expression) in the United States. Commons in Institutional Economics (1934) fills the first 389 pages with a
review of English political economy starting with John Locke.
Why did his students not pick up this interest in historical
pretheories? Bartels suggests they were too busy striving to
develop new theories themselves. I'll advance another hypothesis later. In any case, there must surely be somewhere here
a moral for us today on the proper use of historical pretheory
in the development of theory. Bartels thought so, for he ends
the preface by saying that one purpose of this book, "and not
the least important, [is to] cast upon the subject of metatheory some light gleaned from a retrospective view of efforts
made to advance marketing theory itself" (ibid., p. vii).
Almost surely, the older pretheories are more useful in the
social sciences than would be true in the physical or biological
sciences. However, an essay on this topic will have to wait
for another day.

I would like to turn your attention to another interest of
Bartels, and most of us in marketing: the relevance and relationships of theory in marketing to theory in other social
science disciplines. Bartels' writings begin to develop a
philosophy on this topic in about 1950. In that year he said
that in marketing theory seminars "also will pertinent theories
developed by theoretical economists, accountants, lawyers, and
other social scientists be related to marketing thought" (ibid.,
p. 83). Commenting on another article written in 1950 Bartels
says "to deem marketing a 'science,' however, classifies it as
a . . . discipline in a collective science of social behavior"
(ibid., p. 85). Thus, he is foreshadowing a metatheory that

will unify the theories of the various social sciences into a
"collective science of social behavior." It is this passage
from the book we honor today that is the text for my thoughts.
In that essay, he excludes anthropology, a discipline I will
call upon today, from his list of relevant social sciences,
and he seems to anticipate more of a link with sociology than
with other noneconomic disciplines (ibid., chap. 10). His
article on "Sociologists and Marketologists," published in the
Journal of Marketing in 1959 preceded by five years that by
Glock and Nicosia, "Uses of Sociology in Studying 'Consumption'
Behavior," published in the same journal. In the main, these
forecasts made twenty to thirty years ago appear to have been
amazingly precise. What has not developed is a unification or
a metatheory of social behavior. I have long urged my marketing
colleagues to take on this task or at least to be the theory
broker between the social sciences. We have played this role
to some extent in choice theory, in attitude theory, in exchange
theory, in theories of competitive behavior and its regulation,
and in a few other areas. I want to describe, later, another
area where I believe marketing can play a role in the development of a metatheory of social behavior. But first, I would
like to make explicit, through Bartels' work and my own, the
historical tradition for marketing as a developer of metatheory
in the social sciences.

THE WISCONSIN LEGACY

Bartels' tracing of the development of marketing thought
from the progressive economics department at Wisconsin during
the period from 1890 to 1915 is well known. Students from that
department moved into faculty positions in most Big Ten schools,
in New York, at Harvard, and at California. Paul D. Converse,
of course, is among this group trained in the Wisconsin economics department. Bartels clearly saw and reports to us that
the evolution of the field by these scholars was more strongly
influenced by the cultural and economic environments in which
they worked than by the theory they had learned. His own words
on this point are very insightful.

The principal stimulus to marketing study
at first appears to have been an environment of
progressive economic thought, as illustrated by
the impetus given the study of marketing at
Wisconsin and Harvard. The character of the
contribution made to marketing thought, however,
was less an outgrowth of the economics taught
at a given school than of other environmental
factors. Students working in agricultural
areas devoted themselves largely to study of

38

agricultural marketing. Those in urban and metro-
politan centers specialized more in the marketing
of manufactured goods and in institutional and
technical aspects of marketing [ibid., p. 126].

While I have no way of knowing, I suspect that this understanding of the importance of environment in the development of
theory is something Bartels learned early but that it continued
to crop up unexpectedly to him at various times throughout his
professional career. Commenting in 1970 on an article written
in 1961, he says the article reflected the impact on his thinking of Karl Polanyi and of a year in Greece. "These influences
constituted seeds in the author's thought which germinated in
new views of environmentalism, comparativism, and institution-
alism" (ibid., p. 146).

Now what strikes home to me about that quote is that it
represents exactly the current state of my own thinking regarding the metatheory of marketing. Marketing activity, exchange
activity, any social behavior can only be interpreted with
respect to some theory when the behavior is described in its
environmental context. Indeed, the theory itself is environ-
mentally dependent. Thus, our inability to unify theory across
anthropology, psychology, sociology, political science, law,
economics, and marketing stems, in part, from the fact that
these disciplines do not describe in the same way the environments in which the behavior takes place.

When we in marketing talk of our role as social science
theory unifiers, we are implicitly saying that we hope to
describe the environment in a way that will be acceptable to
all social science disciplines. In other words, we hope to
develop metatheory. I have tried to understand why marketing
seems always to cast itself in this role. The answer, I
believe, is that it always has. Finding a universally acceptable lexicon for the social, cultural, legal, economic environment is exactly what the Wisconsin political economists were
about in 1900. Our roots have cast us in this role. It is our
historical tradition.

If I am correct, then why did those early marketing
scholars in the United States pay so little attention to marketing pretheory writing prior to 1890? My explanation is the
hypothesis just advanced: the society and the economic system.
That is, the environment, prior to 1850 were so different that
U.S. scholars could not recognize the earlier scholarly writings
as being useful. Even the English writings were from the pre-
industrial revolution in a country whose main concern was with
international trade, while marketing problems in the United
States in 1920 were concerned with agriculture and domestic

large-scale manufacturing (Revzan, 1965, pp. 67-73). Further, the United States in the World War I era was in a nationalistic mood. These are exactly the reasons why the less developed countries of the world today have doubts about the relevance of western marketing theory to their societies. A criticism I believe we need to take more seriously.

A movement is now afoot in marketing to recapture the richness of the Wisconsin legacy. The label that seems to be gaining favor for this approach is the "political economy" approach to marketing theory. However, it would be just as appropriate to call us neo-institutionalists. Indeed, the popularity of this approach is appearing in a number of social science disciplines. The motivation behind the approach is to develop a theory for carefully specifying the environmental context in which human activity is studied and thereby to permit the study by social scientists from different disciplines in a fashion that will integrate theory and analysis across disciplines. In organization theory Zald (1970) and Lawrence and Dyer (1980) represent this school of development. In economics, Oliver Williamson's (1975) work fits this mold. In marketing, Stern and his colleagues have long been moving in this direction and use the term political economy. (See particularly Stern and Reve, 1980). Arndt (1979) has also been working in this field. My own efforts are described in a conceptualization I call the "systems/exchange paradigm" (1979, 1980a). In the 1980 Research in Marketing volume, I use social exchange theory to show how a proper respect for environmental context can be used to unify a very important theory in all social science including marketing.

While exchanges would appear to be central to economics, few economists other than Commons have been eager to claim it or attempt to fit general exchange theory into theories of market exchange. Commons found the exchange transaction to be the most useful unit of analysis for investigation (1924, p. 4). In marketing, most of us agree with Kotler (1972, p. 49) that "how transactions are created, stimulated, facilitated, and solved . . . is the generic concept of marketing." Alderson (1965, p. 22) suggests that the transaction--the focus of the negotiation which leads to exchange--is one of two basic "units of action" of a marketing system. He goes on (pp. 83-86) to begin a formal analysis of transactions called the "Law of Exchange." Yet, the progress to date in building a general theory of social exchange has not been rapid. Such a theory will contribute to all of social science, not marketing, psychology,, sociology, or anthropology alone.

It may be useful to describe the differences in perspective between disciplines in a bit more detail. The anthropologist is interested in studying primitive societies with an eye toward understanding the evolution of these to complex societies. The history of development of exchange theory in anthropology dates from at least as far back as 1919.

The writings on exchange in sociology have been criticized as being so general as to be tautological (Emerson, 1976). On the other hand, the paradigm's simple structure permits one to use the framework from the perspective of dyadic social psychology (Thibaut and Kelley, 1959), operant psychology (Homans, 1961), or economic decision theory (Telser, 1972). Our work in marketing (Bagozzi, 1975; Carman, 1980a) suggests that a complete understanding of complex exchanges requires detailed analysis of social, economic, and legal institutions and functions as well as psychology and social mores. In other words, we need a complete description of the environment in which the exchange takes place.

THE ROLE OF COMPARATIVE ANALYSIS

In the 1960s, Bartels' writings reflect that he too had become convinced that the development of a "collective science of social behavior" depended upon a solid understanding of cultural orientation and social structure (Bartels, 1970, pp. 250-253). In order to build a paradigm for such an analysis, he turned to comparative analysis. (This paradigm begins to take shape in chapter 13, written in 1964, and is completed in chapter 18, which was written five years later). The constructs of his comparative analysis framework have much in common with the political economy approach. Bartels in 1964 suggested we define, "the social organization, economic institutions, the nature of markets, marketing functions and functionaries, marketing interactions, and social context" of the marketing system being investigated (Bartels, 1970, p. 199). His final sentence in that article captures the link between development of "a collective science of human behavior" and the environment in which it takes place: "While cultural differences distinguish marketing in different settings, a universality of human nature provides the element of comparability in comparative marketing study" (ibid., p. 204).

In this final section of this essay, I want to turn to one feature of marketing systems in order to make even more firm the link between Commons, Bartels, modern political economy thinking, and the development of a metatheory of marketing. That feature is dispute resolution in vertical channel systems.

Bartels recognized a need to study social control systems, i.e., how the society controls the marketing system. Commons,

41

too, is remembered for his interest in how institutions become the vehicles for social control and individual freedom in a society. For example, in 1934 he developed a thesis rather eloquently that Charles Linblom developed all over again in 1977 in his very successful book, Politics and Markets. Here is one quote from Commons.

> The American problem, if we may derive it from comparison with Russia and Italy, is two-fold: economic and political. We may take two things as fixed and certain for the future. On the economic side is the spread of banker capitalism, on the political side is the sovereignty of the Supreme Court. The things that are unfixed and uncertain are the future of legislatures and the future of voluntary private associations of laborers, farmers, small businessmen, and political parties. Both legislatures and voluntary associations have been abolished in Russia and Italy. Both, we can plainly see, are getting weaker and weaker in America [Commons, 1934, p. 898].

Commons was interested in, perhaps more than anything else, the relationship of conflict, dependence, and order in the face of scarce resources. While he was interested in this subject of the societal level, he also studied conflict resolution at a micro level, i.e., within organizations and system. It was through this analysis that he became convinced that voluntary collective institutions were the best vehicle to minimize internal conflict, or to resolve it at low cost, and also the best vehicle to cause change in other institutions. That is precisely what we neo-institutionalists are about with regard to distribution channels--to shed light on the form of vertical organization that will minimize internal conflict, or its cost of resolution, and at the same time will be efficient in the performance of marketing functions. A reading of Stern and Reve (1980) will make this clear.

Today I want to focus on just one part of this problem, dispute resolution mechanisms among members of the same channel. We all know that all parts of a vertical system may be members of the same corporation or may be composed of a large number of independent firms. Given the characteristics of the member organizations and the markets they serve, not all vertical systems for the same product will have the same structure. A classification of five types of linkages have proved useful in studying this problem: (1) market linkages; (2) leadership linkages; (3) contractual linkages; (4) decentralized, vertically integrated systems; (5) centralized integrated hierarchies.

Each of these five structures deals somewhat differently with conflicts and power among channel members. For example, the leadership linkage differs from market linkage only in that one member of the channel system possesses the power, by trust or coercion, to have other channel members do what the leader wishes. In contractually linked systems, the parties agree to a contract or franchise that spells out the nature of the linkage and specifies how conflicts are to be minimized.

In all three of the first types of linkages, the organizations are under separate ownership and management. Title to product is transferred. In the vertically integrated systems, ownership is common. Carman (1980b) argued that the differences in these five linkage systems are more one of degree than of kind. The analysis of efficiency among these alternative linkage systems requires that one study, among other things, the frequency of disputes and the cost of their resolution in each system. Thus, it is necessary to have a theory for studying conflict resolution in order to develop a theory of channel efficiency.

We do have a literature of dispute resolution. There are only a few aspects of channel disputes that are at all unique. One, of course, is that they are all business disputes, as opposed to domestic or ciminal disputes, as opposed to domestic or criminal disputes. But more interesting is the fact that the parties engage in a very large number of exchange transactions. Their relation is a relatively permanent and continuing one, and there is considerable mutual dependency between the parties. One would aspect that even in the United States where there is a tendency to over-litigate disputes, that there would be a strong preference for resolution techniques that will be face-saving enough to preserve the continuing relationship. It is this aspect of disputes in channel systems that make them particularly interesting.

At least five social science disciplines offer some theoretical advice: law, sociology, political science, anthropology, and marketing. Legal theory is very interested about efficiency in dispute settlement. This interest has led to considerable concern over the present status of the U.S. court system (Fuller, 1978). Thibaut and Walker (1978) have argued that disputes are concerned with determining either truth or equity (distribution of wealth). The adversary procedures we use today are appropriate for deciding the latter but not the former. In channels of distribution, conflicts are of both these types. Channel members argue over the best way to accomplish some goal and they also argue over a fair distribution of the profits. If an adversary procedure is appropriate in the latter case, then perhaps arbitration is a better way to resolve disputes over fact. Arbitration has a long and rather successful reputation in resolving international, domestic commercial and labor disputes (Wetter, 1979). It is specified as the method of resolving disputes in many commercial contracts. However, it has not received much study by marketing scholars.

Sociology, labor relations, and industrial psychology all present theories of dispute settlement that have considerable commonality. This literature also overlaps with the theories of political science of the firm (Tivey, 1978). As such, it usually focuses on worker-management disputes within the firm or on the social control of firms. The former, of course, speaks to the issue of efficiency in conflict resolution within integrated channel systems but does not deal with market, leadership, or contractual linkage systems. Profit sharing, workers' councils, and communes are examples of the topics studied by social scientists working in this area. Of more relevance for us is a model advanced by Kenneth Thomas (1976) in which he suggests that a two-dimensional typology may be useful in determining the behavior of disputants. The dimensions are stake in the relationship and commonality of interest. Depending on where parties are in this typology, they will have a tendency toward one of: avoidance, accommodation, competition, collaboration, or sharing. For disputes between channel members, only avoidance is likely not to be an appropriate response.

Anthropology offers us a particularly rich literature on the disputing process. (For a bibliography through the mid-1960s, see Nader, Koch, and Cox [1966]). This literature seems particularly rich to me because it is cross cultural. The key characteristics of a disputing process appears to be: whether third parties are used, the type of outcome, and the method. The methods available and used universally are: adjudication, arbitration, mediation, negotiation, coercion, avoidance, and "lumping it" (Nader and Todd, 1978). The Thomas model mentioned above could easily be expanded to include all seven of these methods; both theories agree the relationship of the disputants to one another will determine the method of settlement employed.

In marketing channels, as in primative societies, informal dispute settlement methods play a vital role (Assael, 1968; Stern, Bagozzi, and Dholakia, 1977). Marketing scholars have observed, to use the Thomas (1976) typology, that collaboration or accommodation (lumping it) are most common between channel members. Further, as if they were in integrated channels, coercion is common. That is, the inequality of power between the parties causes disputes to be settled by coercion rather than by negotiation or mediation. Thus, the attention in marketing also has turned to the study of relationships between disputants and particularly to the study of power rather than

44

the disputing process. El Ansary and Stern (1972), Hunt and
Nevin (1974), Etgar (1976), and Wilkinson (1979) are representative of the people working in this area. Most of the theories
of power used in this work are based on the conceptualizations
of the sociologists Emerson (1962) and French and Raven (1959).
However, some recent work by another sociologist, Jackson (1975)
may prove even more useful for us in developing theories of
power as a control technique in channels of distribution.

Thus, while my focus here is on dispute settlement, it is
necessary for us to define and measure socially legitimated,
reward, and punishment power potential in order to understand
the methods of dispute settlement employed and their relative
efficiency. It is marvelous to see marketing scholars working
in this area of theory development, for its potential application to real problems facing our profession is great. From a
macro perspective it is we in marketing who should be giving
the world normative models of what kind of linking systems and
what kind of dispute settlement mechanisms are most efficient.
From a public policy perspective, such normative models will
help us understand how to improve both legal processes and
regulatory mechanisms, both currently under considerable
criticism. From a managerial perspective, such models help us
to understand just which linkage structures and managerial
techniques are best in particular channel situations as well as
to understand which disputing process is best.

The industry studies on this subject that have received
the most attention have been concentrated in franchised services.
Fast foods and automobile dealerships have probably received
the most attention. Franchise systems are of particular
interest because power differences tend to be great. Service
industries are of particular interest because the opportunities
for conflict tend to be greater than for products, since conflict can exist over the methods and quality of both production
and marketing. The automobile business is of particular interest because it is a mixture of product and service and because
it has a long history with interesting dynamics. The Automobile
Dealers Association has been active for many decades; super-
dealerships also have helped dealers to build countervailing
power. In a period of a sellers market, the conflict between
manufacturers and dealers led to federal legislation, the
"auto dealer's day in court act of 1956." The lobbying by the
manufacturers to successfully cut the teeth from this act is
well documented (Macaulay, 1966). Since then, softening demand,
oil shortages, and foreign competition have all combined to
weaken the power of the manufacturers and increase the freedom
of dealers (althought they are now much weaker financially).

Thus, while much integration of theories of the disputing

45

process still is required, we have had some merging of these theories and we have some industries that can be studied long-itudinally in order to test such an integrated theory. That theory will surely have relevance to all of the social sciences; it will surely be in the systems/exchange (or political economy or institutional) tradition. However, in order to go from such a theory to a metatheory, I believe we will need to also test cross-culturally this integrated theory of disputing in vertical channel systems. The anthropologist and sociologists are telling us clearly that constructs in these areas are very cultural-ly dependent.

Indeed, a very large portion of what we would include as marketing theory today is culturally restricted to industrial-ized cultures. I believe that is precisely what Bob Bartels is telling us in Marketing Theory and Metatheory. That is, the development of a metatheory of social behavior requires that we develop specific theories of cultural influences. Com-parative research designs are the key to such theory develop-ment. I am in his debt for guidance for the development of the research strategy just outlined for one small aspect of social behavior. I hope our execution of this strategy is at least half as good as his would have been.

REFERENCES

Alderson, Wroe (1965), Dynamic Marketing Behavior, Homewood: Richard D. Irwin, Inc.

Arndt, Johan (1979), "Toward a Concept of Domesticated Markets", Journal of Marketing 43 (Fall), 69-75.

Assael, Henry (1968), "The Political Role of Trade Associations in Distributive Conflict Resolution", Journal of Marketing 32 (April), 21-28.

Bagozzi, Richard (1975), "Marketing as Exchange", Journal of Marketing, 39 (October), 32-39.

Barbon, Nicholas (1960), A Discourse of Trade, Edited by J. H. Hollander, Baltimore: The Johns Hopkins Press, 1903.

Bartels, Robert (1970), Marketing Theory and Metatheory, Home-wood: Richard D. Irwin, Inc.

Carman, James M. (1979), "Where Abstraction: A Systems/Exchange Approach to the Analysis of Health Care Delivery". In Macro-Marketing: New Steps on the Learning Curve. Edited by G. Fisk and R. W. Nason. Boulder University of Colorado

Business Research Division, pp. 47-64.

_____ (1980a), "Paradigms for Marketing Theory,"
Research in Marketing 3, Greenwich: JAI Press, Inc., pp.
1-36.

_____ (1980b), Vertical Systems, Regional Systems,
Substitutability, and Technology: Some Structural Issues."
In Regulation of Marketing and the Public Interest. Edited
by F. E. Balderston, J. M. Carman, and F. M. Nicosia.
Elmsford, N.Y.: Pergemon Press, pp. 203-213.

Commons, John R. (1924), Legal Foundations of Capitalism,
New York: Macmillan Co.

_____ (1934), Institutional Economics, New York:
Macmillan Co.

Converse, Paul D. (1959), The Beginning of Marketing Thought
in the United States, Austin: University of Texas Bureau
of Business Research.

Dixon, Donald F. (1979), "The Origins of Macro-Marketing
Thought." In Macro-Marketing: New Steps on the Learning
Curve. Edited by G. Fisk and R. W. Nason. Boulder: Univer-
sity of Colorado Business Research Division, pp. 9-28.

_____ (1980), "Medieval Macromarketing Thought". In
Macromarketing: Evolution of Thought. Edited by G. Fisk,
R. W. Nason, and P. D. White. Boulder: University of
Colorado Business Research Division, pp. 59-69.

El Ansary, Adel, and Stern, Louis (1972), "Power Measurement
in the Distribution Channel." Journal of Marketing Research
4 (February), 47-52.

Emerson, Richard M. (1962), "Power-Dependence Relations",
American Sociological Review 27 (February), 31-41.

_____ (1976), "Social Exchange Theory", In Annual Review
of Sociology 2. Edited by H. Inkeles, J. Coleman, and N.
Smelser. Palo Alto: Annual Review, Inc., 335-362.

Etgar, Michael (1976), "Channel Domination and Countervailing
Power in Distribution Channels", Journal of Marketing Research
13 (August), 254-262.

French, J. R. P., and Revan, B. (1959), "The Bases of Social
Power", In Studies in Social Power. Edited by Darwin
Cartwright. Ann Arbor: University of Michigan Press, 150-167.

47

Fuller, Lon L. (1978), "The Forms and Limits of Adjudication", Harvard Law Review 92 (353-409.

Glock, C. Y., and Nicosia, F. M. (1964), "Uses of Sociology in Studying 'Consumption' Behavior," Journal of Marketing 28 (July), 51-54.

Homans, G. C. (1961), Social Behavior: Its Elementary Forms, New York: Harcourt Brace & World.

Hunt, Shelby D., and Nevin, John R. (1974), "Power in a Channel of Distribution: Sources and Consequences", Journal of Marketing Research 11 (May), 186-193.

Jackson, J. (1975), "Normative Power and Conflict Potential", In Sociological Methods and Research 4 (November).

Kotler, Philip (1972), "A Generic Concept of Marketing", Journal of Marketing 36 (April), 46-54.

Lawrence, Paul R., and Dyer, Davis, (1980), Challenge to America: The Mutual Adaptation of Organizations and Environments, Harvard Business School manuscript.

Lindblom, Charles E. (1977), Politics and Markets, New York: Basic Books.

Macaulay, Stewart (1966), Law and the Balance of Power, New York: Russell Sage Foundation.

Nader, L., Koch, K. F., and Cox, B. (1966), "The Ethnography of Law: A Bibliographic Survey", Current Anthropology 7, 267-294.

Nader, L. and Todd, H. F., Jr., (1978), The Disputing Process: Law in Ten Societies, New York: Columbia University Press.

Nider, Johannes (1966), On the Contract of Merchants. Translated by Charles H. Reeves, Norman: University of Oklahoma Press.

Revzan, David A. (1965), Perspectives for Research in Marketing: Seven Essays, Berkeley: University of California Institute of Business and Economic Research.

Schwartz, George (ed.) (1965), Science in Marketing, New York: John Wiley Sons, Inc.

Stern, L. W., Bagozzi, R. P., and Dholakia, R. R. (1977), "Mediational Mechanisms in Interorganizational Conflict". In Negotiations, Edited by D. Druckman, pp. 367-388.

Stern, Louis W., and El Ansary, A. I. (1977), Marketing
Channels. Englewood Cliffs: Prentice-Hall Inc.

Stern, Louis W., and Reve, Torger (1980), "Distribution
Channels as Political Economics: A Framework for Comparative
Analysis", Journal of Marketing 44 (Summer), 52-64.

Telser, Lester G. (1972), Competition, Collusion and Game
Theory, Chicago: Aldine-Atherton.

Thibaut, J., and Kelley, H. H. (1959), The Social Psychology
of Groups, New York: John Wiley and Sons.

Thibaut, J., and Walkter, Laurens (1978), "A Theory of Procedure", California Law Review 66 (May) 541-566.

Thomas, Kenneth (1976), "Conflict and Conflict Management",
In Handbook of Industrial and Organizational Psychology.
Edited by M. D. Dunnett, Chicago: Rand McNally, pp. 889-935.

Tivey, Leonard (1978), The Politics of the Firm, New York:
St. Martin's Press.

Wetter, J. G. (1979), The International Arbitral Process:
Public and Private, Vol. II, Dobbs Ferry, N.Y.: Oceana
Publications, Inc.

Wheeler, John (1931), A Treatise of Commerce (1601), New York:
Facsimile Book Society.

Wilkinson, Ian F. (1979), "Power and Satisfaction in Channels
of Distribution", Journal of Retailing 55 (Summer).

Williamson, Oliver E. (1975), Markets and Hierarchies, New
York: The Free Press.

Zald, M. W. "Poltical Economy: A Framework for Comparative
Analysis", In Power in Organizations, Nashville; Vanderbilt
University Press, pp. 221-261.

BARTELS' METATHEORY OF MARKETING: A PERSPECTIVE

Shelby D. Hunt, Texas Tech University
Kenneth A. Hunt, Virginia Polytechnic Institute

Interest in the area of marketing theory has grown tre-
mendously in the last few years. There have been several books
published on the subject (Zaltman 1973; Hunt 1976; Bagozzi
1980), several special conferences on marketing theory spon-
sored by the American Marketing Association, a special plea by
the editor of the Journal of Marketing for more theoretically-
oriented articles, and the American Marketing Association is
planning another special conference on marketing theory in
1982. Unfortunately, such high interest was not always the
case. After a spurt of interest in the subject in the 1950's
and early 1960's, there was a period of time when very few
marketing academicians were actively involved in attempting to
theorize concerning marketing. Robert Bartels was one of the
"handful" who kept marketing theory alive during it's "Dark
Ages."

Bartels' work in the area of marketing theory culminated
in a seminal book entitled Marketing Theory and Metatheory
published by Richard D. Irwin, Inc. in 1970 under the sponsor-
ship of the American Marketing Association. This volume represents a compendium of Bartels' past work in the area of marketing theory and, also, some original articles prepared especially for the book. The article which sets the tone for the entire
volume is the first article entitled "Marketing Metatheory."
The article develops seven axioms of marketing metatheory
which explains Bartels' philosophical perspective on theory and
provides a focus for the rest of the volume. The purpose of
the present paper is to examine the seven axioms comprising
Bartels' metatheory of marketing. Before doing so, it would be
helpful to examine the concept "metatheory."

METATHEORY

As far as this writer can determine, Bartels was the
first marketing author to use the term "metatheory." According
to Bartels, a metatheory of marketing is "a theory of the characteristics that marketing theory should possess and by which
it should be judged." In contrast with a theory which is a
"summary or considered conclusion reached after analysis and
synthesis of information," a metatheory is a "theory concerning
theories and theorization." Thus, according to Bartels a

metatheory relates "not to the content of marketing theory but to it's form."

As proposed by Bartels, the term "metatheory" is an exceptionally broad concept relating to both the philosophy of science and the sociology of science with respect to theory development. This perspective is consistent with Zaltman et al (1973) who proposed that metatheory is "the investigation, analysis, and the description of (1) the technology of building theory, (2) the theory itself, and (3) the utilization of theory."

In contrast with marketing writers, philosophers of science usually restrict the term "metatheory" to a particular theory, rather than theories in general. The Encyclopedia of Philosophy (1967) defines metatheory as "the metamathematical investigations relating to a given logistic system." Woodger also discusses the distinction between theory and metatheory:

> In the first place it is most important to keep constantly in mind the distinction between a theory which deals with a certain subject matter (in the ways in which a particular biological theory deals with some aspects of animals or plants) and a theory which has the given Theory as it's subject matter. The theory which has a given theory T as it's subject matter is called the metatheory of T.

Although Bartels use of the term "metatheory" is broader than mainstream philosophy of science, extending the use of the term beyond a particular theory would seem to be useful enterprise. The balance of the paper will deal with the seven axioms proposed by Bartels as a metatheory of marketing.

IDENTIFICATION

The first axiom of Bartels' metatheory is that "theory proceeds from a concept of it's subject and should be consistent with it." Stated conversely, a theory "should not be built upon uncertain or conflicting concepts of a subject." Indicating that this axiom is "seemingly obvious and hardly disputable," Bartels suggests that "lack of precise subject identification has introduced confusion into marketing thought by minimizing the importance of difference in expositions of marketing."

Axiom one addresses the fundamental issues raised by the "broadening the concept" debate. That is, is marketing a

(1) technology, (2) social process, (3) set of activities engaged in only by profit-seeking institutions? The implications for theory development in marketing are enormous. If the conceptual domain of marketing is limited to it's technological aspects, then theory development in marketing should aim at normative theory rather than positive theory. Whereas positive theory seeks to describe, explain, predict and understand marketing phenomena, normative theory seeks to provide a systematic set of decision rules to guide marketing decision makers.

If marketing is to be viewed as primarily a social process, this too would impact on marketing theory. Social process theory development would tend to focus on the relationships between marketing and other social processes in society. Such theories would be typically very "macro" in orientation. The issue of whether marketing includes both profit-oriented institutions and nonprofit-oriented institutions impacts on the theoretical problem of exactly what phenomena marketing theory seeks to explain. Given a "transactions" perspective of marketing, is marketing theory seeking to explain only economic transactions or, also, noneconomic transactions?

Although it may be premature to proclaim a universal consensus on the "broadening" issue, I believe there is an emerging consensus that the appropriate domain for the concept "marketing" should include the micro/macro dimensions, positive/normative dimensions, and profit sector/non-profit sector dimensions. However, we must recognize that this very broad conceptualization of marketing and marketing phenomena, magnifies the difficulty of developing a general theory of marketing.

In conclusion, the first axiom points out some very fundamental issues in constructing marketing theory. The discipline of marketing has made substantial strides in the last decade in addressing these issues. Nevertheless, the direction that the discipline has gone in addressing these issues has magnified the task and significantly increased the difficulty of generating marketing theory.

BASIC CONCEPTS

The second axiom of Bartels' metatheory for marketing is that "theory is built upon basic concepts derived from the concept of the subject and from related scientific disciplines." Although Bartels recognized that many of the concepts in marketing theory are drawn from other scientific disciplines, the basic concepts are always consistent with the basic concept of marketing held by the theorist. The concepts used in theory

52

generation will be significantly influenced by whether the theorist considers marketing to be primarily a technology, or a social process, or a set of economic activities.

Consider the developments in the area of channels of distribution theory. As Stern and Reve (1980) have pointed out, theorists who viewed marketing as primarily a technology focused on a traditional problem-solving approach to channels of distribution theory (C.F., Gattorna 1978; McCammon and Little 1965; McCammon, Bates and Guiltinan 1971). Technologically-oriented channels of distribution theory used such concepts as pricing procedures and tools to motivate channel members. Considering marketing to be primarily an economic activity, suggests using "efficiency" as a primary dependent variable and focusing on costs and functions of channel members. Considering marketing as primarily a social process encouraged channel theorists to examine for relationships among such concepts as power, conflict, and satisfaction. Recently, Stern and Reve (1980) have suggested approaching channels of distribution from a political economy approach. They contend that channels of distribution theory must consider the internal economy and polity of distribution channels in conjunction with the external economy and polity of the environment. "The contribution of the political economy framework is the explicit insistence that economic and sociopolitical forces not be analyzed in isolation."

There is a fundamental lesson to be learned from axiom two: when we unnecessarily delimit the concept of marketing, we also unnecessarily limit the kinds of concepts that we will recognize as being useful in explaining and predicting marketing phenomena.

INTRACONCEPT DIFFERENCES

The third axiom is that "by subdivision of basic concepts, their range and qualities may be shown in intraconcept differences." Bartels proposes that concepts "have two types of diversity: differences of kind, and differences of degree." Bartels discusses the subdivision of concepts by noting that "subconcepts constitute a refinement of the categories of thought, making possible the statement of hypotheses with greater exactitude and precision."

In axiom three Bartles examines the problems of taxonomy in marketing. This writer must agree with Bartels that taxonomical issues in marketing are both extremely important and extremely difficult. Developing adequate taxonomies is a crucial phase in the creation of marketing theory. Current

53

thinking in taxonomy suggests that there are two fundamentally different procedures for classifying phenomena: logical partitioning and grouping (Harvey 1969). Logical partitioning is sometimes called "deductive classification," "a priori classification," or "classification from above." The procedures known as "grouping" are often called "inductive classification," "ex post classification," or "numerical taxonomy." The essential difference between logical partitioning and grouping procedures is that with the former the classificational schema is always developed <u>before</u> the researcher analyzes any specific set of data. In contrast, when using grouping procedures the researcher generates his schema only <u>after</u> he or she analyzes some specific set of data. With logical partitioning the researcher <u>imposes</u> a classificational system on the data; with grouping, the researcher lets the data suggest the system. Both kinds of procedures are used in marketing and both have their strengths and weaknesses.

INTERCONCEPT RELATIONSHIPS

The fourth axiom of the metatheory is that "concepts in a dependent-independent relationship are the bases of explanation or prediction." Bartels proposes that "the purpose of theorization is twofold: to predict and to explain." Further, he indicates "the establishment of [dependent-independent] relationships is essential to the construction of theory."

The relationships that Bartels refers to as "dependent-independent" are commonly referred to as "law-like generalizations" in the philosophy of science literature. The notion that law-like generalizations are absolutely necessary for prediction, explanation, and theory is very consistent with modern philosophy of science. Law-like generalizations are necessary for theory development since all scientific theories, by definition must contain law-like generalizations (Rudner 1966).

The necessity of law-like generalizations for scientific explanation is also consensus philosophy of science. There are three generally accepted models of scientific explanation: (1) deductive-nomological, (2) deductive-statistical, and (3) inductive-statistical (Hempel 1965). With deductive-statistical and deductive-nomological explanations the explanandum is logically deduced from a set of initial conditions and a set of law-like generalizations of either <u>statistical</u> or <u>universal</u> form. With inductive-statistical explanation the explanandum is <u>inferred</u> from a set of laws of statistical form. In all three cases of scientific explanation there must be law-like generalizations in the explanatory model. Attempts to explain

54

phenomena without the use of law-like generalizations have been unsuccessful.

All law-like generalizations have the basic form of "if x occurs then y will occur." That is, all-law generalizations have the basic form of generalized conditionals. Nevertheless, not all generalized conditionals are law-like generalizations. Only generalized conditionals which satisfy three criteria are considered law-like: (1) empirical content, (2) nomic necessity, (3) systematically integrated (Hunt 1976). The empirical content criterion suggests that only those generalizations which relate, directly or indirectly, to real world phenomena can be considered as law-like. The second criterion, nomic necessity, provides that the theorist must show that there is some kind of "necessary connection" among the concepts. That is, simple, accidental generalizations are not to be considered law-like. Needless to say, demonstrating a "necessary connection" is easier said than done. Finally, "the systematically integrated" criterion suggests that isolated empirical regularities are not law-like. The generalizations must be incorporated into a body of theory before they are considered to be law-like.

GENERALITY OF RELATIONSHIPS

The fifth axiom is that "theory based upon presumed relationships is valid to the degree that those relationships have generality." Bartels suggests that "the merit of the theory lies in the validity of its predictions, in the coincidence of its explanations with experience." He goes on to indicate that "the generality which gives credence to theory is evident in repetition of the interaction of related factors, in their congruence under different circumstances, and in their consistence with other theory."

The fifth axiom echoes the modern empiricism of philosophy of science. That is, the ultimate test of any theory is the validity of its predictions. Stemming from the work of the early logical positivists, modern philosophy of science holds that any proposition which purports to represent how the world is organized must be amenable, either directly or indirectly, to empirical tests.

It is important to point out the empirical testing of propositions does not presume that every concept in the proposition has an empirical counterpart in the real world. Rather, the content of the proposition as a whole must make some kinds of predictions about phenomena which do have real world referents.

DIVERSITY OF THEORIES

The sixth axiom provides that "as theory bears the mark of the marketing theorist, individuality and diversity are normal characteristics of theory." Bartels suggests that "when a theory is not subjectable to precise confirmation, as it is not in marketing, the criteria for theory evaluation must include subjective as well as objective determinants of its quality." He concludes that "the criteria of self-knowledge of the theorist, his insight, sincerity, and intellectual integrity, as well as the realism and usefulness of his point of view these, too, are criteria by which theory in a social field must be appraised."

This writer has substantial concerns about axiom six. It seems to be saying that the validity and acceptability of a theory in marketing is to be judged not only by how well it describes, explains, and predicts, but also, on the basis of who proposes it. It would appear that the acceptance by marketing of such as axiom could generate a great deal of mischief in our discipline. Although simple minded "appeals to authority" may play a legitimate role in theology, such appeals are generally unacceptable in science.

THEORY AND EPITHEORY

The seventh axiom is that "all theories of a discipline, however diverse, should be embraceable, implicitly or explicitly, in a general theory, either by grouping or by synthesis." Bartels indicates that "the unification of diverse theories takes place in two ways: (1) through integration or combination of differences, and (2) through the resolution or dissolution of differences."

It is well recognized that Professor Bartels has long believed that a general theory of marketing is (1) highly desirable, (2) attainable, and (3) in fact already exists (Bartels 1968). Very few marketing academicians would doubt the desirability of a general theory of marketing. However, many would question whether it currently exists. Nevertheless, no one doubts that a general theory of marketing is an objective well worth striving for. As the poet Browning once said, "man's reach should exceed his grasp, else what is heaven for?"

CONCLUSION

In this analyst's judgment the metatheory proposed for marketing by Professor Bartels stands up very well under close scrutiny. With rare exceptions his metatheory is very consistent with modern philosophy of science. The axioms, both individually and collectively, provide a useful perspective for anyone seriously interested in developing theory in marketing. Bartels' metatheory represents a significant step in pushing all marketing academicians toward more rigorous theory development.

REFERENCES

Bagozzi, Richard P. (1980), Causal Models in Marketing, New York: John Wiley and Sons, Inc.

Bartels, Robert (1968), "The General Theory of Marketing," Journal of Marketing, 32 (October).

_____ (1970), Marketing Theory and Metatheory, Homewood: Richard D. Irwin, Inc.

The Encyclopedia of Philosophy (1967), New York: MacMillan Publishing Co., Inc.

Gattorna, J. (1978), Channels of Distribution, European Journal of Marketing, 12, 7, 471-512.

Harvey, David (1969), "Explanation of Geography," New York: St. Martin's Press.

Hempel, Carl G. (1965), Aspects of Scientific Explanation, New York: The Free Press.

Hunt, Shelby D. (1976), Marketing Theory: Conceptual Foundations of Research in Marketing, Columbus: Grid Inc.

McCammon, B. C., A. D. Bates and J. D. Guiltinan (1971), "Alternative Models for Programming Vertical Marketing Networks", in New Essays in Marketing, G. Fisk, ed., Boston: Allyn and Bacon, 333-358.

_____ and R. W. Little (1965), "Marketing Channels: Analytical Systems and Approaches," in Science in Marketing, G. Schwartz, es., New York: John Wiley and Sons, 321-384.

Stern, Louis W. and Torer Reve (1980), "Distribution Channels as Political Economies: A Framework for Comparative Analysis", Journal of Marketing, 44 (Summer), 52-64.

Woodger, Joseph H., (1970), "The Technique of Theory Construction," in Foundations of Unity of Science, Volume 2, Otto

Neurath, ed., Chicago: The University of Chicago Press, 449-532.

Zaltman, Gerald, Christian R. A. Pinson and Rienhard Angelmar (1973), <u>Metatheory and Consumer Research</u>, New York: Holt, Rinehart and Winston.

CONSUMER BEHAVIOR: A CRITICAL
ASSESSMENT

James F. Engel
Wheaton Graduate School

In 1956 I had the unusual privilege to enroll in the last
two classes taught at the University of Illinois by Paul D.
Converse. I was unprepared for his style, to say the least.
His folksy humor disarmed me into thinking that this would be a
"snap course". My midterm grade was the lowest of the 30 in the
class, and that fact probably did more than anything else in my
professional career to drive home the need for careful, analytical scholarship. P. D. later became my dear friend. Probably
more than anything else, I learned from him a historical perspective on our field that has served me well to this day.

I mention this bit of background simply to say that nothing
could mean more to me than receipt of the Converse Award. This
truly reflects both his professional and Christian influence on
my life, and I hope that I will always be able to live up to
this honor. To my peers who considered me worthy of this, I
can only express my heartfelt thanks.

In this short paper, I will try to express some thoughts
on the subset of the field of marketing which I know best--con-
sumer research. Hopefully my remarks here will not unduly re-
peat those given in Fall, 1980 when I was awarded a similar
honor given by the Association for Consumer Research--designa-
tion as one of the first two Fellows in Consumer Behavior
(Engel 1981). Undoubtedly there will be some overlap between
the two papers, because it is hard to express largely the same
thoughts in differing ways.

THE DEVELOPMENT OF A DISCIPLINE

One thing I learned when reading the multitude of sources
recommended by P. D. Converse covering such names as Ward,
Weld, Copeland, and Cox (I was one of the few who actually read
this stuff--I had not yet been told how to cope with the demands of graduate school), it became clear to me that the consumer is the focus of marketing. Earlier writings, of course,
appeared in the era when there was an excess of demand over
supply, with the result that primary focus was placed on production and distribution. Yet the consumer was not ignored.
Copeland and others (Copeland 1920) were not unaware of the
psychological thinking of their day. Such terms as rational and

emotional motives really were reflective of the importance
placed on motive as a variable in general psychology (Murray
1938). We can look back at this point in time and view such
thinking as being a bit naive, but the blame for that lies
squarely in the behavioral sciences of the time.

The consumer moved to the center, so to speak, in the days
after World War II when suddenly supply exceeded demand and
marketers found themselves with some bulging warehouses. One
of the contributions to the marketing literature of that time
is at long last receiving just recognition in this symposium.
That, of course, is the concept of market segmentation given
its first systematic exposition by Wendell Smith (Wendell T.
Smith). I can well remember when he spoke at the University of
Illinois about 1957 and explained market segmentation. Clearly,
it changed the focus of much of our thinking, and segmentation
lies at the very bedrock of consumer behavior research today.
Peter Drucker also contributed much in <u>The Practice of Manage-
ment</u> by stating that service to the consumer is the one central
goal of business.

It was about this time, the late 1950's, that some were
beginning to see what the behavioral sciences might contribute
to marketing. Bob Ferber and Hugh Wales were instrumental in
my taking a minor in social psychology, but this was only a con-
tinuation of a direction initiated by my mentor at Drake
University, Marty Zober. Others were doing the same elsewhere.
A few of these names are Don Cox, Hal Kassarjian, Bob Pratt,
Jim Myers, and, of course, a number of others who began to write
on various behavioral subjects in the middle and late 1960's.

All of a sudden, in short, it became the "in thing" to have
a background in both marketing and behavioral science. I just
happened to be one of the early ones. It really was more by
accident than by design. We were treated as being a bit strange
and perhaps even dangerous in our places of employment. The
University of Michigan tolerated me for a few years, but I must
say that I found the confines of Ohio State to be a vast improvement, especially after Kollat and Blackwell joined me. Now
it was three oddballs rather than one.

Most of our early attempts were nothing more than what Jack
Jacoby has called "the theory of the month club" (Jacoby 1978).
I did my thing with the theory of cognitive dissonance (Engel
1963). It's interesting how quickly some trivial research got
published and led to some professional recognition for me.
Fortunately, that research has gone into oblivion where it be-
longs, but I do not apologize for it. It was a serious attempt
to apply a promising psychological theory to consumer behavior,
and that's the way a new discipline begins. In a sense it was

a fishing expedition for some of us, but what other choice did
we have? My concern now is that the theory of the month club
has not seen its demise, judging by the papers we still see for
example on attribution theory and person perception theory. In
my opinion, these theories have contributed little or nothing
to what we already know; yet they appear and are applauded as
if new breakthroughs have occurred. Maybe it's time for some
of us to be a bit more demanding on what we allow to be published and count toward academic promotion. Just making a
"refereed journal" should not be an end, in and of itself. But
enough of that!

Consumer Behavior Approaches Adolescence

As I have said elsewhere (Engel 1981), I think we can
safely say that the whole field of consumer behavior research
has gone beyond its infancy and now has approached a pretty
healthy state of adolescence. Let me point to some reasons
lying behind this evaluation.

First, let's be straightforward about one central point:
consumer behavior shares a common foundation with marketing--
it is an engineering discipline as Ithiel de sola Pool pointed
out some years ago. In other words, various disciplines coa-
lesce with the goal of finding solutions to applied problems.
It is not a science or discipline in and of itself.

There are some who would like to view consumer behavior as
a unique discipline, whereas in reality it is the study of decision making and buying in the economic arena. Considerable
use is made of theory, but this is borrowed, by and large, from
the various subfields within social and cognitive psychology.

Given this fact, what progress has been made in the past
20 years or so? There is no denying that the whole field has
been given a boost by the fact that a young professor today
must either be "behavioral", "quantitative", or both. Hopefully it also would be good if he or she knew a bit about traditional marketing also, but that probably sounds old fashioned.
Riding the crest of the fad as we have, a sophisticated literature has developed. It is fair to say, in my opinion, that no
other arena of human behavior has received such widespread and
systematic empirical investigation. Most of our research has
assumed, falsely I believe, that consumer behavior is high in-
volvement--i.e. there is considerable ego involvement and extended problem solving behavior. Nevertheless, much of what we
know about high involvement decision behavior in all phases of
life has its roots in this discipline. I have been able to bor-
row profitably many of the concepts and methods in my current
field of interest--religious problem solving behavior.

61

There has been considerable theory development, probably epitomized by the large scale models such as those developed by Howard and Sheth (1969) and Engel, Kollat, and Blackwell (1968). But there are a number of reduced form models which have led to considerable useful research. Most notable here is Fishbein's extended model (1975) and the various theories of information processing (choice heuristics) given their clearest exposition by Bettman (1979) and Wright (1973). Once again, however, let me reiterate that these models all make use of variables and concepts from the various underlying behavioral sciences focused, of course, in this particular arena of behavior.

Probably one of the most noteworthy aspects of a maturing field is the onset of replication. Many consumer researchers quake today when they hear the term "multi-attribute models", because we beat this one pretty hard over a number of years. Nonetheless, the amount of replication which has been done has established the multi-attribute model as an important bedrock in research on high-involvement consumer behavior. As tiresome as this may seem to outsiders, progress cannot occur any other way. I for one welcome it, because it was sadly absent only a few years ago. All somebody had to do then was to publish something that sounded "behavioral" and was sufficiently vague that no one understood it. That automatically meant that it was a profound contribution. Shortly thereafter, it would find its way into our basic marketing books as a proven principle. Could that, by the way, explain some of the short-lived popularity of Dichter and so-called motivation research? For many of us, the first years of our careers were devoted to putting motivation research to death. Replication, then, is a definite sign of growing maturity.

Consumer Research Contributions to Parent Disciplines

It is fair to say today that consumer research no longer is viewed with disdain by social psychologists and others. Many of us had to live through the "slings and arrows of outrageous fortune" in a sense as we were the victims of their barbs. "How could you dirty your hands and corrupt yourself in that way." Today we find researchers from all disciplines flocking into our ranks. Quite frankly, I think the biggest reason is that there is money to be made here. Interesting isn't it how academic purity caves in under economic realities?

Consumer research has come into respectability for other reasons, however. I feel that our comprehensive models have shown many an ivory tower theorist a thing or two about how meaningful theory can be built. These models are careful constructions of variables and linkages designed in such a way as to explain behavior. There are few counterparts in the behavioral science literature. In other words, we have shown some

62

ways in which theoretical models can be used in a sophisticated manner to explain and predict behavior. In this sense, we take a back seat to no one.

I have already referred to the replication which is underway and the growing quantity of sophisticated research. Frankly, it is my opinion that consumer researchers have done far more with the Fishbein model that anyone else. We have not been afraid to subject it to some pretty demanding inquiry which goes beyond college sophomores forced to participate in a psychology experiment. I could give many other examples as well. What I am saying about this is that researchers today have the conceptual and methodological sophistication to do some mighty good work which is filtering back into the "halls of ivy". We have not reached our zenith in this respect by any means as Jack Jacoby has pointed out, but real progress has been made (1978).

Probably consumer researchers are just now on the brink of our greatest potential area of contribution--low involvement behavior. Only recently, thanks largely to Krugman (1979), have we recognized that much consumer behavior is low involvement. In a nutshell, this means that there is low relevance. It just does not make much difference what brand a person buys. Is it really that important, for example, to have Charmin in the bathroom? We used to refer to this kind of product as "convenience products". The point is that consumers hear about it in some way, probably through television, and then buy it without problem solving. In short, they form beliefs and attitudes <u>after</u> <u>purchase</u>, not before, as we have long assumed in our high-involvement extended problem solving models which hypothesize the so-called "hierarchy of effects" (belief→attitude → intention→purchase). Leo Bogart said it well some years ago:

> Perhaps the main contribution that advertising research can make to the study of communications is in the domain of inattention to low-key stimuli, as exemplified by the ever increasing flow of unsolicited and unwanted messages to which people are subject in our over communicative civilization (Bogart 1969).

In short, low involvement theory focuses on behavior when people really just don't care all that much what choice they make. In that sense, consumer research probably has a distinct contribution to make to our parent behavioral sciences which, quite understandably, have pretty much avoided this category of behavior. Can you imagine a reputable psychologist studying toilet paper purchasing?

The Dichotomy Between Academe and Application

Yes, I think it is fair to say that consumer behavior as a discipline has come into its own, but there is a controversy within our own ranks which cannot be avoided. The question is a simple one: does the business world lead the academe or is the reverse true? In other words, one would hope that those of us primarily employed in academic ranks would be plowing some of the basic ground in such a way that what we uncover will diffuse into the world of the user. Unfortunately, the opposite seems to be the case. There will be some disagreement with me on this point I am sure, but I do not think academic researchers have much of a record when it comes to <u>relevance</u>. Relevance is defined here somewhat narrowly as addressing problems analytically which are of concern to those who must contend with consumer issues either from the perspective of marketing or perhaps from the broader dimensions of consumer welfare.

Every paper which we present in our erudition has that obligatory section entitled "practical implications". Every few years Roger Blackwell and I must wade through this literature to uncover that which should find its way into those ever-present revisions. We both agree that the straining some of our colleagues undertake to find practical implications for their work is absurd. It is my contention that our research agenda gets pretty far out of whack. In part this reflects the reward systems of our academic institutions which by and large give accolades if something is published in a refereed journal. It doesn't matter much what is said. I for one am a strong advocate for completely turning the emphasis here. The issues investigated should be evaluated at the outset for relevance. This is not to argue for a narrow pragmatism which focuses only on trivial strategic concerns. But somehow, somewhere we must be able to demonstrate that practitioners ultimately can benefit from our profundity. We still are plagued by the theory of the month club. Once again I say to the advocates of attribution theory and person perception theory, prove your case that these latest "hot buttons" advance the state of the art. The burden is on you, not on the rest of us.

I have long pleaded for some degree of partnership between academic researchers and those from the applied world. Here and there this happens, but still we see educators and practitioners meeting separately within the American Marketing Association. Certainly that ought to tell us that we are operating on separate agendas. Must this continue forever?

By the way, some will take issue with me here on my opening statement that the business world has led the academe rather than the reverse. I will stick to my guns. Take a look at the methods or concepts which have received the lion's share of

64

attention in recent years (with the single exception of multi-attribute models). Most would mention psychographics and conjoint analysis right off the bat. Here we see the leadership of Bill Wells and Paul Green who have a foot in both camps but have developed their thinking primarily from an applied perspective. With these few exceptions, I am afraid that academic consumer researchers pretty much talk to ourselves. Disagree? Just count the number of practitioners who come to our sessions at either the American Marketing Association or the Association for Consumer Research!

LOOKING TO THE FUTURE

In a sense, I guess I am saying that the state of the art is a pretty "mixed bag". Really this is to be expected, however, given the relative youth of our discipline. We have come a long way, and there is no denying that fact, and I am most optimistic for the future. It probably is necessary in a paper like this to play the role of pundit and predict the future. I do that with some temerity, but I will comment on some issues which we cannot avoid if progress is to be made.

Broadening Our Disciplinary Focus
With few exceptions, consumer researchers receive their training in psychology--social psychology, cognitive psychology, psychometrics, and so on. Only rarely does one encounter someone like Zaltman (1979) who has broken that mold and dared to wander into such uncharted waters as sociology. It's time to broaden these perspectives.

In my opinion, our greatest short coming is the almost total neglect of cultural anthropology. Sheth (1979) and a few others have lamented our incredible naivete when it comes to understanding consumer behavior cross culturally. In the last ten years, I have had the privilege of leading management seminars for Christian workers in 38 countries of the world and have lived outside the United States for a total of about one year during that time. I have come to see that our western thinking is ethnocentric to the hilt. We somehow assume that individualistic hierarchy of effects models of problem solving behavior are normative for the world. Nothing could be further from the truth. This subject could be treated in an entire book and still not do it justice. Just let me say this: it's time to bring cultural anthropology into our balliwick. If we avoid doing it, we risk being seen as irrelevant by those throughout the world. I speak from first hand experience on this. Just ask the missionaries what happened to them until they took the very step I am advocating here.

65

Placing a Priority on Reliability and Validity

A number of us have been contending for years that our research methodology rests on some shaky foundations. Only here
and there is reliability and validity taken seriously (Churchill
1979). For the most part we use paper and pencil tests which
may have face validity only and proceed as if there is something
magic in our findings. In reality, our findings may be a dis-
torted artifact of our methods. This issue cannot be swept
under the rug. Fortunately, there are many voices now being
raised, and we should see improvement.

Some, by the way, seem to feel that "number crunching"
can make up for methodological inadequacy. The more we do in
the way of multi-variate analysis, clustering, and so on, the
better. That does help get an article published in the Journal
of Marketing Research, I suppose, but number crunching is not
an end in and of itself. What if the hypotheses being investigated are trivial and irrelevant? What if there are obvious
biases in the questionnaires and tests? These questions are
far more important than the sophistication of the analytical
techniques.

A Concern for Morality

Kotler argued cogently in the last Converse Awards Symposium that a mature discipline must take the issue of morality
and values seriously (1979). To be quite honest, that is almost
totally lacking in the whole study of consumer behavior. In my
opinion, no discipline could be more amoral (not immoral) in its
development to this point.

Here are just a few issues which ought to give us pause for
some serious reflection:

1. What happens if we get to the point in our under-
    standing of information processing that it will be
    possible to circumvent the individual's abilities
    to screen out unwanted messages?

2. Physiological measurement has pretty much reached
    the point where it is now possible to analyze con-
    sumer response without recourse to verbal question-
    ing. Do we have the right to invade the sanctity
    of another person's life in that way?

I have a much deeper concern, however, which has recently
been brought into sharp focus by Yankelovich (1981). He under-
scores the obvious pervasive value in western culture which
calls for virtually unrestrained consumption, no doubt based on
the rarely questioned assumption that a high and rising standard
of living is the key to happiness. To use his words: "Our

culture and our economy are on opposite courses: while the
culture calls for freedom, the economy calls for constraint."
(Yankelovich 1981). He is saying that unrestrained consumption
is no longer possible in a world of limited resources. This is
hardly a startling conclusion, but where, if ever, do consumer
researchers discuss such issues? Our greatest problem may be
to de-stimulate demand, and it's high time we recognize this
fact. This is a moral issue, by the way, because many will
argue that individual freedom should never be interfered with.

Then we face such ticklish issues as this: is it right to
sell products which have an obviously nonbeneficial effect on
the user? Cigarettes are an example (Ok cigarette companies,
barrage me now with your contradictory propaganda). If people
want them, shall we just go ahead? Some will say, sure. I for
one will draw the line pretty clearly because I feel researchers
must first and foremost look to the best interest of the individual. Admittedly decisions such as this must be based on a
working value structure. The point is that it is about time we
bring the whole issue of values into our considerations.

Clarifying Our Agenda for Research
The last point I would like to make goes back to earlier
comments on relevance. As matters now stand, most of our conferences in this field consist pretty much of a scattering of
topics. If we are good enough number crunchers and can cite
enough esoteric theory, we can probably get on the program. But
so what? When we are all through, what exactly have we learned?
There are a few marvelous exceptions to this tendency such as
special topic sessions on low involvement theory and so on. We
need more of this. Somehow, someway we must collectively come
to grips with research priorities. There are bound to be some
wide differences in perspective here, but let's at least discuss
it. Otherwise we will muddle along showing a breakthrough here
and there but mostly spinning our wheels. It is here where
dialogue between responsible academicians and practitioners is
a must.

A CONCLUDING WORD

There would have been a time in my life where receipt of
this award would have been the absolute highlight of my career.
It still means a great deal to me for the reasons mentioned at
the outset. But I would be very remiss if I did not give credit
where it is due. About 16 years ago, my wife and I discovered
for the first time that there is more to life than material
success. It was then that we began to take our Christian faith
seriously. In every sense of the word I found my values changing. A sense of meaning and purpose filled a growing vacuum.

My professional life took on a new dimension as I centered all I did around service to something beyond my self--my Lord Jesus Christ. With true sincerity, I accept this award and give all the credit and glory to him.

REFERENCES

Bettman, James R. (1979), An Information Processing Theory of Consumer Choice, Reading, MA: Addison-Wesley.

Bogart, Leo (1969), "Where Does Advertising Research Go From Here?", Journal of Advertising Research, vol. 9, (March), p. 6.

Churchill, Gilbert A., Jr. (1979), "A Paradigm for Developing Better Measures for Marketing Constructs," Journal of Marketing Research, vol. 16 (February), pp. 64-73.

Copeland, Melvin T. (1920), Marketing Problems, New York: A. W. Shaw Company.

Engel, James F. (1963), "The Psychological Consequences of a Major Purchase Decision," in W. S. Decker, ed., Marketing in Transition, Chicago: American Marketing Association, pp. 462-475.

_____ (1981), "The Discipline of Consumer Research: Permanent Adolescence or Maturity?", in Kent B. Monroe, ed., Advances in Consumer Research, vol. 8, Ann Arbor, MI: Association for Consumer Research, pp. 12-14.

_____, David T. Kollat and Roger D. Blackwell (1968), Consumer Behavior, New York: Holt, Rinehart and Winston, Inc. This has since appeared in three editions, and the fourth edition will be published in 1982 under the authorship of Engel and Blackwell.

Fishbein, Martin and Icek Ajzen (1975), Belief, Attitude, Intention and Behavior: An Introduction to Theory and Research, Reading, Mass.: Addison-Wesley.

Howard, John A. and Jagdish N. Sheth (1969), The Theory of Buyer Behavior, New York: Wiley.

Jacoby, Jacob (1978), "Consumer Research: How Valid and Useful Are All Our Consumer Behavior Research Findings? A State of the Art Review," Journal of Marketing, vol. 42 (April), pp. 87-96.

Kotler, Philip (1979), "A Critical Assessment of Marketing Theory and Practice," in Alan R. Andreasen and David M. Gardner, eds., <u>Diffusing Marketing Theory and Research: The Contributions of Bauer, Green, Kotler, and Levitt</u>, Chicago: American Marketing Association, pp. 1-15.

Krugman, Herbert E. (1979), "Low Involvement Theory in the Light of New Brain Research," in John C. Maloney and Bernard Silverman, eds., <u>Attitude Research Plays for High Stakes</u>, Chicago: American Marketing Association, pp. 16-23.

Murray, H. A. (1938), <u>Explorations in Personality</u>, New York: Oxford University Press.

Sheth, Jagdish N. (1979), "The Surpluses and Shortages in Consumer Behavior Theory and Research," <u>Journal of the Academy of Marketing Science</u>, vol. 7 (fall), pp. 414-427.

Wright, Peter L. (1973), "The Cognitive Processes Mediating Acceptance of Advertising," <u>Journal of Marketing Research</u>, vol. 10 (February), pp. 53-62.

Yankelovich, Daniel (1981), "New Rules in American Life: Searching for Self-Fulfillment in a World Turned Upside Down," <u>Psychology Today</u> (April), pp. 35-91.

_____, "New Rules in American Life," p. 43.

Zaltman, Gerald and Melanie Wallendorf (1979), <u>Consumer Behavior: Basic Findings and Management Implications</u>, New Wiley.

TEACHING AND RESEARCHING CONSUMER BEHAVIOR:
REFLECTIONS ON THE CONTRIBUTIONS OF A PIONEERING WORK

Donald H. Granbois

Since the initial entry into the academic marketplace of
Consumer Behavior by Engel, Kollat and Blackwell in 1968, the
number of published empirical studies of consumer behavior has
increased many fold. As in most of the applied behavioral
sciences, this inventory of studies includes some works of
questionable value, as well as a few reports of research that
have had important impact on our understanding of the consumer.
The widespread initial acceptance and continued adoption of the
EKB textbook has undoubtedly been one of the important influences of this vast outpouring of consumer research. The book's
contribution to the explosive growth of consumer research over
the past decade, both as a stimulus encouraging practitioners
and academics to undertake research and as a determinant of the
direction and form of research, provides a solid basis for recognizing Jim Engel with the Paul D. Converse Award.

I am especially pleased and honored to be invited to provide comments on this occasion. As a friend of Jim's since our
days here at the University of Illinois as graduate students,
as an occasional co-author with Jim, as one of the reviewers
secured by Holt, Rinehart and Winston to react to the original
EKB manuscript, and as one of the first adopters of the text,
I have followed Jim's career--and the processes of adoption and
diffusion of the text--with a great deal of interest. As one
of Jim's fellow students in the last two courses taught by P.
D. Converse, I have some understanding of the strong influence
of P. D. as a researcher, writer and teacher on Jim's work. I
suspect that P. D. would be very pleased to know that the career
he helped influence has been recognized with this award.

Most of you in this audience are well aware of the many
ways Jim Engel has contributed to the advancement of the field
of Marketing besides his leadership role in developing the EKB
text. Jim's role as initiator and organizer was instrumental
in getting the Association for Consumer Research started, his
impact on graduate students at Ohio State has been considerable,
his research articles and other texts and readings books have
been widely read, and his many appearances at professional conferences have always reflected Jim's deep concern for the discipline of Marketing. Still, the EKB text is probably the most
important product of Jim's career. The book has truly made a
major and long-lasting impact on the development of Marketing
thought and practice. Through its widespread adoption and

70

appearance in countless footnote references in the works of other writers the book is probably the greatest single source of Jim's strong reputation in the field of Marketing.

In discussing this contribution, I will first briefly show why the book has had such an important impact on the study and practice of Marketing. I will then identify and attempt to assess the importance of several factors and influences present in the 1960's that led to the original plan of the EKB text. Finally, several of the specific impacts and influences of the book on consumer research will be identified, together with some predictions and prescriptions for future directions in the field.

Contributions of the Text: An Overview
At least three aspects of the EKB text account for its important impact on Marketing. The work provided a framework for the systematic study of consumer behavior and thus helped establish the scope of a discipline that was emerging in the 1960's as a result of several influences. Unlike some writers in other fields, Jim and his co-authors deliberately structured their book around a clearly distinguished framework--the EKB model--and wrote chapters to elaborate upon each of the major components of the framework. While the elements of the model were not original with the authors, the combination and organization of elements was logical, easily understood and encouraged the reader to discover important researchable questions about the behavior of consumers.

While the idea of a comprehensive model was not original with EKB (Andreasen, Nicosia and Howard and Sheth published models during the mid and late 1960's too), the second aspect of the book--its synthesis of research findings--contributed importantly to its impact. While the level of empirical documentation of the various elements of the EKB model was pretty uneven in 1968, the discussion presented what evidence could be found, together with a balanced critique and evaluation and usually some attempt at interpretation in terms of managerial implications. I have always marvelled at the authors' ability to present a research synthesis at a level that was at the same time acceptable and understandable by undergraduates and of value to academics and practitioners interested in using the model to guide an actual research study.

The final aspect of the book's impact was its design for use as a textbook rather than as a scholarly monograph. This format contributed importantly to the dissemination of its content. Although there were some pre-1968 courses in consumer behavior offered, these for the most part were based on collections of readings, which are notoriously difficult for all but

the most experienced and skillful instructor to use effectively. The appearance of the EKB text therefore encouraged and
facilitated the growth of formal courses in consumer behavior.
Many of today's practitioners in Marketing were given a solid
introduction to research on the subject via EKB. The impact of
the book on Marketing academics has undoubtedly been important
too. As graduate students and teachers, many current academic
researchers in consumer behavior had their first exposure to
the field in courses featuring the book. This exposure has
certainly influenced these researchers' problem choice and concepts and frame works used, and the book has provided an initial
literature review for many dissertations and faculty research
projects.

Such has been the impact of the framework offered by the
EKB text that no importantly different text has yet appeared,
despite the fairly large number of competing books that have
been recently published. Many of these texts present the EKB
model directly, and all benefit from the pioneering literature
review and synthesis faithfully brought up to date in succeed-
ing EKB editions.

Influences Contributing to the EKB Text

While contemporary writers often attribute the early growth
of consumer research to the impact of scholars trained in the
behavioral sciences who began to teach in business schools in
the 1960's, the academic study of marketing research was already well-established and served as an important input to the
birth of consumer behavior as an academic field. Jim Engel was
a product of this tradition, having been influenced strongly by
Professor Martin Zober during his undergraduate studies at
Drake University. Professors Lloyd DeBoer and Hugh Wales at
Illinois were popular and influential teachers of courses in
marketing research, and Wales, in particular, impressed upon
Jim the need for methodological rigor while introducing him to
much of the better literature in the field. Wales later super-
vised Jim's dissertation research.

The Journal of Marketing in the 1950's and 1960's published articles on survey methods and in-store experimental
techniques and occasionally reported results of applications
of these methods. Marketing research academics were at the
forefront in the movement to critically examine the methods and
findings of the "motivation researchers" practicing during the
period, and it was the widespread academic rejection of motivation research that encouraged those interested in understanding
the consumer to seek alternative and more acceptable frameworks
and methodologies.

72

Although the research methods and publication formats used were not the same as those now widely employed, many early Marketing academics had a strong empirical orientation. To some extent, this was born out of necessity; training in Economics was found inadequate to provide the "real world" flavor required in teaching courses in Marketing. P. D. Converse used to say that he was forced to observe and measure the behavior of Marketing practitioners and consumers, since when he started teaching Marketing there weren't any books available on the workings of the main marketing institutions and the behavior of the buyers and sellers involved in them. This research orientation, especially strong at the University of Illinois when Jim studied here, pre-dated the "behavioral science" invasion of business schools by some years.

Jim was one of the first Marketing doctoral students to study seriously one of the behavioral sciences as part of his program. His work in motivation, attitude, learning and perception in the Psychology Department at Illinois not only facilitated writing good chapters on these topics for the EKB text, but encouraged his view of human behavior as goal-directed, evaluative and deliberative, concepts deeply influential in developing the EKB model of the consumer decision process.

His early faculty years at the University of Michigan introduced Jim to pressure for publication and saw the execution and publication of Jim's well-known cognitive dissonance study of recent auto purchases. The essentially negative findings of the study were in the same vein as earlier studies applying psychological models (notably Franklin Evans' attempt to relate auto brand choice to personality). The interpretation seemed to be that consumer studies borrowing concepts and models from the "pure" behavioral sciences without any integrating framework or attempt to assess the applicability of the borrowed concept or model to the specific phenomenon under investigation are likely to contribute little towards furthering our understanding of consumer behavior.

During this period, Jim co-authored his Promotional Strategy textbook with Hugh Wales and Martin Warshaw. The rejection by his publisher's editor of the "behavioral" content of several chapters presenting psychological concepts and research findings relevant for understanding audience response to Marketing Communications left Jim with a partial basis for a new text dealing exclusively with consumer behavior.

The 1963 American Marketing Association Educators' Conference was the outlet for the presentation of summary versions of extended literature review and synthesis papers prepared by several researchers (Ray Bauer, James Carey, Donald Cox, Jim

Engel and myself). The review papers illustrated very clearly that there were several research traditions in the behavioral sciences whose apparent applicability to the study of consumer behavior was very good. The experience may have also discouraged Jim, who served as project director, from entering into further co-authorship relationships with people scattered at different locations, given the difficulties we all experienced in communicating and deciding on common formats and styles. At the same time, enthusiasm for the project among presenters and audience members proved that the time was ripe for systematically mining the behavioral science literature for frameworks and findings useful in studying consumer behavior.

Finally, Jim's move to Ohio State, with its traditionally strong emphasis on textbook writing, facilitated developing the book. Co-teaching a doctoral seminar with Roger Blackwell and David Kollat (who was an enthusiastic student of the decision making literature while a doctoral student at Indiana) gave further impetus to the project. While it is difficult for an outsider to assess the relative contribution of each co-author, Jim's role seems to have been that of senior author in a true sense. A doctoral student in the seminar, Larry Light, is acknowledged by the authors as the originator of the first version of the EKB model which found its way, in modified form, into the first EKB edition. Thus, all the ingredients came together to facilitate the development and introduction of a successful, innovative and influential book.

Specific Impacts, Predictions and Prescriptions

While drawing heavily from the behavioral sciences (especially psychology), the EKB text had a strong marketing management emphasis. Advertising applications were given particularly strong development, perhaps reflecting Jim Engel's earlier teaching and text-writing experience. This emphasis on relevance for management, on viewing consumer behavior at least in part as response to "external" stimuli including many controlled by marketing management, is consistent with the marketing research courses and literature of the 1950's and 1960's as well as the marketing management focus which gained strength in general marketing courses during that period. This managerial focus is strong in the consumer behavior discipline today. The Association for Consumer Research remains dominated by Marketing academics, and articles in professional journals and proceedings volumes usually contain obligatory paragraphs at the beginning and end in which the relevance of the problem statement and findings is interpreted for managers.

Both the initial and subsequent comprehensive models serving as the framework for the EKB text start with the familiar Stimulus $\longrightarrow$ Intervening Variable $\longrightarrow$ Response logic from psychol-

74

ogy, firmly establishing the discipline in the micro, individual psychological mode. Virtually all subsequent texts, models, and a large proportion of consumer research studies have followed this example. The literature presenting models, theories and research on individual behavior were substantially better developed at the time the book was written than was the comparable literature on group behavior, and this material was more easily taught and learned. As a consequence, however, group variables including even interaction and conflict patterns within the family were relegated to the role of influences and points of reference partially determining individual behavior. Literature reflecting group processes such as that on family roles and interpersonal communications and influence was reviewed but could not be integrated into the comprehensive model.

The construct "stages of decision making", incorporated as the "black box" element of the EKB model, was an attractive device for organizing discussion of behavior which intuitively seemed to be a sequential process. Paul Lazarsfeld had persuasively argued the merits of such a view of behavior, and the EKB model seemed an excellent guide to both "morphological" and "analytical" investigation. Widely used in other disciplines, the stage model fit perfectly with the notion that human behavior is largely purposeful, a view of the consumer which contrasted sharply with the psychoanalytical model of the motivation researchers strongly discredited by Marketing scholars.

Several important aspects of consumer behavior and related research certainly relate well to the stages of decision making model. "Problem recognition" as a sub-process, for example, seems to be an appropriate framework for viewing the planning process which consumers may enter into before undertaking major purchases. Studies of housing, automobile and major household durable purchases are strengthened by the notion that one or more precipitating and/or enabling circumstances may trigger awareness of a need for action. Postulating an "internal search" process heightens our awareness of the need to study consumers' past experience and the nature and extent of stored information. "External search" highlights the importance of the shopping process and alerts us to the fact that consumers in this mode are unusually receptive to stimuli having current relevance for their needs. "Alternative evaluation and choice" permits an integration of attitude and choice models, and forces recognition that consumers' perceptions of alternative choices in terms of criteria salient to them determine choice, not product features or advertising themes favored by sellers. The feedback following outcome psotulated by the phase model seems to correspond to post-consumption evaluation, wherein expectations and perceived performance are compared and the resulting degree of satisfaction/dissatisfaction may trigger further behavior.

Unfortunately, the "Stages" model provides such an intuitively strong fit with the behavior we observe in ourselves and others that we may be falsely lead to believe that consumer purchases always reflect _decisions_, where choice occurs within a field of two or more performance criteria. Such is the appeal of the model, in fact, that consumer researchers have never seriously challenged the model in studies structured to pit the decision stage model against competing explanations for consumer purchase behaviors. In fact, research has been heavily concentrated on the "mental processes" specified by the model rather than on the behaviors--actual purchasing and consumption of goods and services--that might be expected to be given far greater prominence in a discipline generally thought to be "applied" in nature.

The flexibility of the stage model, its apparent ability to describe virtually every kind of individual and group behavior, is at once its strength and a deterrent to full understanding of specific behaviors. The high level of generality of the model leads one to see common dimensions across widely varying behaviors. For example, although many quite different sub-processes are exhibited by consumers as they become activated and begin to initiate processes which eventually culminate in purchase, by classifying all such events as Problem Recognition we tend to overlook many subtle differences. This very abstract view of consumer behavior that has resulted from the application of a single model is in sharp contrast to that of "motivation research" studies. In these studies, every product was seen as a distinct bundle of meanings and characteristics, and many very specific behaviors involved in the art of using a product (and the consumer's reported and imputed feelings and gratifications flowing from these behaviors) were reported in great detail. In motivation research, the specific product and the many unique behaviors associated with it was the dominant variable; individual differences among consumers were given little attention. (Indeed, the in-depth, small sample techniques in use did not permit valid exploration of such individual differences.) In contrast, consumer research structured around the highly abstract decision making model virtually ignores product differences, but makes much of individual differences and their socio-economic, life style, personality and other correlates.

Since the model's scope is limited to a single decision, the EKB discussion seldom considered interactions among the many purchasing and consumption behaviors consumers make. Individual products and services in reality are purchased and consumed as parts of complex systems, and decisions affecting how scarce resources (disposable income and time) are to be allocated among competing uses by their very nature require at least some consideration of trade-offs and interactions among decisions. Choices between <u>generic</u> products and the allocation of funds among larger spending categories are not easily modelled with the EKB model, and thus are given little attention by the authors. Unfortunately, few consumer researchers have given much consideration to research questions growing out of these generic choice and allocation tasks either.

Finally, the decision model is static, even though consumer behavior is obviously an on-going process, with many of the benaviors involved repeated many times over the course of an individual consumer's life cycle. Because of the difficulty one would face in attempting to make a dynamic version of the process model understandable to beginning students, Jim Engel and his co-authors were probably wise not to attempt such a task. Even the notion that decision processes, when repeated for the same product over time tend to shift from extended to habitual problem solving was given very slight coverage in the EKB text. Their decision to include two chapters on models dealing with change over time—I refer here to those chapters on diffusion and on brand loyalty—without attempting to integrate those chapters with the EKB model has, however, perhaps had the effect of discouraging such attempts at integration by anyone. Brand loyalty and diffusion studies have continued to follow their respective traditions and virtually no one has studied how decision <u>processes</u> change over time with experience.

To their credit, Jim Engel and his co-authors have been quite willing to change and refine both the EKB model and the emphasis and interpretation given the research literature surveyed as they prepared the second and third editions of the text. In the book itself and elsewhere, they have been frank in their criticism of both the scope and method of the consumer research they have reviewed. To add emphasis to some of the issues they have discussed, as well as to summarize some of the points made earlier in this paper, several needed research directions are listed briefly to close the comments offered today.

(1) Studies pitting the decision stage model against competing models are needed. Alternative models include conformity, imitation, hybrid processes involving both choice and non-choice mechanisms, and automatic application of rules or preferences acquired in early childhood. It seems likely that each of the competing models (and perhaps others) may be found to apply to consumer behavior, giving rise to the need for further exploration of the incidence and nature of non-choice

mechanisms underlying behavior. Children and other first-time
user groups will be important subjects for such research. The
idea of studying special strategic populations is not new; actual applications in consumer research are still pretty rare,
however.

(2) Deep process studies of two or more person group interactions are badly needed. Interaction process analysis
schemes and frameworks are plentiful in other disciplines, and
single subject protocol analysis methods may prove to adapt
very well in this application. Such studies might well be more
realistic than those using individual subjects, given the apparent frequency of joint consumer behaviors. They also overcome much of the lack of reality of pure protocol analysis,
where subjects are required to verbalize what otherwise would
be silent mental processes.

(3) Experimental studies of behavior in controlled settings should be much more frequently done by academics. Both
in-store manipulation (where much consumer information processing appears to take place) and experimentation in special CATV
communities, where mass media channels are structured so as to
permit experimental manipulation of broadcast and print mes-
sages, are becoming more common in research done by practitioners. Academics need to learn how to do such research and
should have many good ideas about models, concepts and issues
that can best be addressed in such settings. Achieving this
application by academics will require much more cooperative
research involving academics and practitioners.

(4) Researchers need to break away from the over-worked
issue of brand choice and study broader issues of household
management of resources. Generic product choice, budget allocation methods, and other topics probing the interactive nature
of consumer purchasing and consumption behavior need to be explored.

(5) Far more attention needs to be paid to product as a
major variable explaining variations in consumer behavior.

(6) More explicit concern for changes in behavior over
time needs to be shown. Despite a flurry of interest in longitudinal research several years ago, little has been done to
really explore how consumer processes change with repetition.

JAMES F. ENGEL:
TWENTY YEARS OF CONTRIBUTIONS TO CONSUMER BEHAVIOR

W. Wayne Talarzyk
Roger D. Blackwell

In most situations of this type the common thing is to express appreciation for the honor of being able to comment on
the award recipient's career and contributions. Not wanting to
thwart tradition--so be it. We are pleased to have been selected to reflect on Jim Engel's many significant contributions
to the field of marketing in general and consumer behavior in
specific. Professor Engel is certainly a well deserving recipient of a Paul D. Converse Award.

But beyond the trivial as Jim might say, we also appreciate
the opportunity to say publicly some of the things we have
shared with some of you privately. Namely, the many ways in
which Jim has impacted us personally. Many in the field of
consumer behavior have benefited from knowing Jim and being
able to work with him on specific projects.

The two of us, however, have been even more fortunate.
Through various research projects, university affiliations,
writing activities, professional and academic conferences, and
a very important strong sharing of mutual Christian beliefs, we
have benefited more than most from knowing and interacting with
Jim.

So let us begin on a relatively personal note. Jim, we
want to thank you very much for the many ways in which you have
helped us with our personal careers and our perspectives on the
world. Thank you for sharing your ideas, your enthusiasm, your
motivations, and most importantly your time with us. We have
greatly benefited by having you as a close working colleague
and personal friend. Thank you.

Our role today, however, is a broader one. In a sense, we
represent all of our marketing colleagues in being here to ac-
knowledge and comment on the contributions Professor Engel has
made and the impact he has had on our academic discipline. To
help do that we want to organize our observations and thoughts
around four basic areas:

1. An overview or organization of his writings and
   other contributions.

2. A specific focus on the work Consumer Behavior
   on which this award is primarily based.

3. Comments on Jim Engel the person, his motivations and objectives.

4. A future orientation as to types of contributions Professor Engel will continue to make to consumer behavior.

We tried to think of some clever title for this review since Jim has enjoyed a play-on-words in the titles of some of his articles. For example: "Motivation Research, Magic or Menace" Parts I and II (Engel 1961), "Linear Programming: Boon or Boondoggle" (Engel and Warshaw 1963), and "Great Commission or Great Commotion" (Engel 1977). Some of the ideas we discussed included: "EKB: A Model or Monstrosity", "Consumer Behavior: Contributions or Contradictions", and "Jim Engel: Thinker or Stinker".

In the final analysis, fortunately, none seemed appropriate for such a distinguished individual. We concluded with the more mundane title, "James F. Engel: Twenty Years of Contributions to Consumer Behavior".

WRITINGS AND CONTRIBUTIONS

Professor Engel has published more than sixty articles and research reports and twelve books. Space does not permit a detailed description of all of these writings but it is of value to briefly summarize them along the lines of several interest streams. The following sections are positioned pretty much in chronological order based on when Engel first began working and writing in the given area.

Consumer Behavior
Engel's first published articles were the previously mentioned "Motivation Research, Magic or Menace", Parts I and II (1961). His career approach to issues came through loud and clear in the first article:

> If motivation research has so much to offer, then why isn't it more widely accepted in the business community? This is a valid question because for various reasons, many managers and marketing researchers alike have failed to achieve a true understanding of what motivational research can do for them (Engel 1961, p. 30).

Throughout over thirty articles and five books in the area of consumer behavior Engel has consistently focused on taking the concepts and explaining them in such a fashion that they can be understood by managers and marketing researchers alike. His guiding objective throughout this area of endeavor has been to

blend theory and reality into an actionable state. He has a-
chieved his objective more often than not.

Early in his career, Engel also focused on the concept of
cognitive dissonance and published pioneering work in the area
(1963, 1965). This empirical work involved proper integration
of social psychology concepts and methodologies into an understanding of the ways consumers behave with the ultimate objectives of improving advertising and marketing strategies. In
the area of cognitive dissonance, he also displayed an attribute not always present in researchers, the willingness to re-
vise his views when his research and that of others indicated
the need to do so.

Engel also analyzed and evaluated various methodologies of
gathering and interpreting consumer behavior information. Among
these efforts included various ways of obtaining consumer data
(Engel and Wales 1961 and 1962, Engel 1962) along with an approach to studying consumer behavior over time (Engel and Granbois 1965).

In the mid sixties, Engel teamed up with two young, assis-
tant professors, Roger Blackwell and David Kollat, at The Ohio
State University to begin an academic program focusing on consumer behavior. That three-member team along with a set of
highly motivated doctoral students began to discuss, evaluate,
clarify, and develop the basic model which eventually led to the
well-known series of books on consumer behavior. More on that
series of books will be presented later.

Promotional Strategy
     In the early sixties, many behaviorally oriented marketers
were finding their primary teaching opportunities in advertising, promotion, and communication types of courses. Engel was
no exception. But in that arena he elected to participate in
the development of a new type of textbook, one which borrowed
concepts, theories, and methodologies from social psychology
and made them operational in the marketing area of communications. That textbook, Promotional Strategy (Engel, Wales and
Warshaw 1967) is now in its fourth edition.

Once again, Engel and his colleagues focused on taking
relevant concepts and presenting them in an operational format.
In the preface to the fourth edition of Promotional Strategy
the on-going focus is made clear.

     As a basic text, Promotional Strategy: Managing
     the Marketing Communication Program differs somewhat
     from many similar works. It builds on a rigorous
     base of consumer behavior and then proceeds to treat
     advertising, sales promotion, reseller simulation,
     personal selling, and other communication tools as

part of an overall promotional mix.... The approach throughout is to develop fundamental considerations as background and then to focus on managerial issues and problems. Problems are viewed through the eyes of the promotional manager, and major emphasis is placed on understanding the factors that affect promotional divisions and mold managerial strategy (Engel, Wales and Warshaw 1967, preface).

In addition to the textbook and accompanying casebook, Cases in Promotional Strategy (Engel, Talarzyk and Larson 1971), Engel also conducted research in several specific areas of promotion. With others he examined linear programming as a tool for allocating advertising expenditures (Engel and Warshaw 1963 and 1964), looked at brand preference and its influence on perception of persuasion (Engel and Stern 1965), and the influence of package copy claims on product evaluations (Engel, Dean and Talarzyk 1972). As with his other research and writings, Engel continued to focus on pragmatic issues.

Christian Publications

Throughout his career, Engel has also written articles and books in the general area of marketing (Engel, Beckman and Davidson 1967) and the specific area of market segmentation (Engel, Fiorillo, and Cayley 1971 and 1972). He has also applied his understanding of promotional strategy and consumer behavior to the pharmacy area of self-medication products (Engel, Knapp and Knapp 1966, Engel 1966).

In 1965, Engel's reputation as a researcher, author, and teacher was being well established. But as he gained the success and reputation he had sought, it seemed as though something was still missing. His own words reflect his position and what happened:

> I have only given part of the picture on the changes which occurred in my life years ago, and I would be remiss by not filling in the remainder. I also had to face the deeper question of whether or not recognition and achievement really is a sufficient foundation for life itself, because it became increasingly non-satisfying. Fortunately my wife and I began a great adventure 15 years ago as we began for the first time to take our Christian faith seriously and place this eternal dimension at the center of our lives. That adventure continues to this day. It has led to a profound change in personal motivation as I have been freed to focus on basic issues from a perspective of some well-formed and functioning values which have their roots beyond myself (Engel 1981, p. 14).

Engel began to take his understanding of consumer behavior and promotional strategy and apply it to the area of Christianity. His first non-secular publication was "Campus Chaos: God's Opportunity" (Engel 1969). He continued his primary work in consumer behavior and promotional strategy but it was becoming clear that Engel was more and more interested in applying his expertise to an area he felt very close to: the effective communication of the basic truths of Christianity.

In 1972, he left Ohio State to join the faculty of Wheaton College. There Engel greatly expanded a graduate program in Christian communications and began to work with a variety of different Christian organizations to apply his secular knowledge of how consumers behave.

He has now published some 25 articles and three books including the widely circulated, What's Gone Wrong with the Harvest (Engel and Norton 1975) and his latest book, Contemporary Christian Communications: Its Theory and Practice (Engel 1979). Engel has clearly practiced what he preaches: take the relevant concepts in consumer behavior and promotion and apply them to appropriate areas where they can help solve the problems confronting marketers and other communicators.

Organizing
It would be inappropriate to overlook Engel's abilities and contributions in terms of getting things done. He saw the need for an organization that would cut across disciplines, that would allow for more effective exchange of ideas and results, and that would ultimately enhance our overall understanding of consumer behavior.

Toward that end, he along with several colleagues, organized a Workshop on Consumer Behavior which was held at Ohio State in the summer of 1969. Close to forty researchers met and discussed papers of mutual interest at that workshop. As the workshop drew to a close, Engel led a discussion on the need for an organization to provide on a regular basis the types of experiences and insights that had developed during the previous few days.

The response was overwhelming and a new organization was born--The Association for Consumer Research. In the best sense of a marketer, Engel had identified a need and set about the task of bringing about a solution to that need.

CONSUMER BEHAVIOR TEXTBOOK

As stated previously Professor Engel has made many contributions to the field of marketing in general and consumer behavior in specific. The Paul D. Converse Award, however, is being presented primarily for his work on the textbook Consumer Behavior. That book is now in its third edition with the fourth edition coming out early next year.

Since both of us are closely aligned with Jim, both professionally and personally, we are somewhat concerned about our ability to present a dispassionate and objective look at his work on the various editions of Consumer Behavior. We decided, therefore, to let the text speak for itself to some extent and to rely heavily on reviews and comments of other academicians.

The preface to the first edition stated the direction of the text along with four basic objectives, which, by the way have not changed across the four editions:

> This book seeks to meet the needs of both practitioners and those who have a more theoretical interest in the consumer. Its objectives are (1) to explore and evaluate an extensive body of research evidence from marketing and the behavioral sciences; (2) to advance generalizations or propositions from this evidence; (3) to assess the marketing implications of the various processes and facets of consumer motivation and behavior; and (4) to pinpoint areas where research is lacking.... The basic method of exposition is a conceptual model of consumer motivation and behavior. This model specifies relevant variables that shape consumer action and the ways in which each fits into a large scheme (Engel 1968 preface).

With this excerpt from the preface and other observations gleaned from a careful review of the first edition (and subsequent ones) several key points can be made about the model around which the text is structured.

1. It is a framework for integrating research. The discipline of consumer behavior has many partial theories, or bits and pieces of information about how consumers behave. This model is an attempt to bring the insights together in such a fashion that ultimate consumer behavior might be better understood.

2. The model was never intended to be a predictor of behavior. Instead it was designed more as a pedagogical aid, a map to guide students of consumer behavior systematically through the varied disciplines of sociology, psychology, marketing, and some economics.

84

3. It was also designed to serve as a think piece for marketing programming, an organized way to consider consumer influences on distribution, product development, promotion, and pricing. It was hoped that organizations could and would use the model to evaluate existing marketing programs and generate new ones.

4. At no point was it designated as "the" model of consumer behavior. Instead it was presented as "a" model, with suggestions that it could be revised and added to as new insights in consumer behavior became available. In fact, as can be seen in later editions of the text, the model has been significantly modified as research in consumer behavior has progressed.

Well, the question is, how did the marketplace respond to this new textbook in a relatively new discipline? The answer—quite well. It became widely adopted and many courses in consumer behavior were built around its chapter title. Dick Teach had the following observations on the text:

> This book is the first _real_ textbook in consumer behavior and is an important step in making the field a basic part of the marketing process.... The generous use of the model helps the reader keep track of the complex buying process and the specific variables being considered one at a time. It reminds the reader that the individual is a complex system and the variables are conditional in nature and not independent.... It does not meet the needs of making the consumer behavior concepts operational for the practitioners in the field. However, it is an excellent, easy to read, and understandable textbook viewing purchase behavior as a broad concept (Teach 1969).

Jim and his coauthors must have been pleased with the review with the exception of the observation regarding its ability to meet the needs of the practitioner. The second edition, however, significantly dealt with that issue.

> This edition also differs from the first edition in that we have placed greater emphasis on problems of measurement and application of generalizations to practical problems. As a result, the book has a distinctly pragmatic focus. We are of the opinion that, while the study of consumer behavior is valuable in its own right as an academic discipline, it is of far greater importance to center on the problems faced by those who must make decisions based on an understanding of the consumer (Engel, Blackwell and Kollat 1973 preface).

The textbook continued its success in the second edition. More schools began to add courses in consumer behavior and Engel, Kollat, and Blackwell's book was the choice for the majority of the courses. The reviews again, were quite positive.

> This welcome second edition of a major textbook in the field continues the high level of the first. All aspects of consumer behavior are updated and rather thoroughly treated.... Comprehensive, lucid, conceptual, yet sufficiently pragmatic for any marketing practitioner.... The esoterics of consumer behavior need to be brought down to the realm of practicality--and this the authors have done admirably well (Hartley 1974).

The ten years from 1968 to 1978 yielded a dramatic increase in the research on consumer behavior. With this additional knowledge the authors made major changes in their model. The text was also modified in certain areas to help clarify issues in operationalizing and testing the model.

> The basic method of exposition is a conceptual model of consumer behavior that has been revised in some important aspects since the 1973 edition. The present version bears only a scant family revision to its 1967 forefather, reflecting the dramatic growth in knowledge since that time. The revised model highlights the decision process more sharply and represents, we feel, a step forward in specification of the linkage between variables. We have also been more cognizant of the need for more precise definitions, formalization of variables and their hypothesized linkages, and clarification of the problems of operationalization and testing (Engel, Blackwell and Kollat 1978 preface).

It appears as though the third edition is still the standard against which all other texts are evaluated. The text is still widely used by graduate and undergraduate courses in spite of the numerous books in consumer behavior which have been introduced in recent years. The following two quotes are helpful to put all editions of the text in perspective along with specific emphasis on the third edition.

The first quote is from Hal Kassarjian's presentation at last year's ACR conference which honored Professor Engel and Professor John A. Howard as the first two Fellows of the Association for Consumer Research. The second quote is from Carol Scott's recent review of six consumer behavior tests in the Journal of Marketing.

> The culmination of that effort was the first true textbook in the field, Engel, Kollat, and

Blackwell's consumer behavior trilogy. Now in its
third edition, and the fourth being conceptualized,
that text has unquestionably become the standard work
in the field by which all other texts, course outlines,
and course content are compared and categorized.
Throughout the land, courses in Consumer Behavior
were introduced with the EKB Table of Contents as the
outline. What was left for other authors and publishers of texts was to attempt to carve out a small market share below or around the EKB positioning, for it
is still the standard work in the field (Kassarjian
1981).

The Engel et al. book is written at the most
sophisticated level, with the others written in
simpler and more entertaining style. If I had to
choose between the five books discussed thus far,
however, Engel et al. would have a slight edge.
Although I do not agree with its position on all
issues, and there are features of the other books
that I wish had been incorporated in it, it still
appears to be the most complete (Scott 1981).

Time marches on and so does the need for yet another edition of Consumer Behavior. Such an edition will be forthcoming
next year, and if the past is any indication of the future it
will, in all probability, continue to be the overall leader in
the field. In this forthcoming edition of the text, the model
will have minor revisions but there will be two separate versions to reflect new insights into and dimensions of consumer
behavior.

While the basic model in this edition bears only
a scant family resemblance to its 1968 forefather,
it has only been changed in minor ways from the 1978
version. What is new this time around is the distinction between high involvement behavior and low involvement behavior. Both are radically different,
with the result that we are using two models for the
first time. The earlier EKB model explained only
high involvement behavior (Engel, Blackwell and
Kollat 1982 preface).

JIM ENGEL: THE PERSON

At the 1980 annual meeting of the Association for Consumer
Research, Jim Engel was honored as one of the first two Fellows
in Consumer Research. Officially, the award was presented "In
recognition of his singular contribution to the systematic study

87

of consumer behavior".

That recognition plus the information presented so far today, helps us to understand what Jim has done for our discipline, and he has done a lot, to be sure. But what else should
be said about him as a person; or as the common questions go,
what makes Jim tick or what makes him run?

Jim is a man in a hurry. It is important to quickly indicate that this is not meant in a negative way. He is in a
hurry to get on with that which needs to be done, not necessarily to finish a project by cutting corners.

On one bright Saturday morning, Jim was observed mowing
his lawn with a hand mower. When asked if he was on an ecology
kick or concerned about conserving energy he quickly gave negative responses. Instead, he replied that the gasoline powered
mower wouldn't go fast enough for him.

So Jim is a man in a hurry, but in some instances this
characteristic may have caused people to misunderstand him. At
times, Jim may seem to be impatient or too outspoken on a given
issue. As people get to know Jim, however, they realize that
such attributes are admirable given the issues he is concerned
about.

Jim is willing to take a stand and be counted, to let his
feelings be known, to challenge others to get them to think
about what they are doing or should be doing, about the contributions they can or should make. But at the same time, Jim is
equally willing to back up his actions with genuine concerns for
others and displays a willingness to reach out to others and
give a helping hand or encouraging word when they are most
needed.

Jim is an individual with a high moral standard, requires
that his own work achieves that standard, and encourages others
to do likewise. As an example of that encouragement, in accepting the Fellow in Consumer Behavior award he challenged our
discipline to devote more attention to the long-run social and
moral implications of our understanding of consumer behavior.

I cannot imagine a discipline that is more amoral than
ours. Only rarely do we address the social implications of what
we are doing. What are the long run implications, for example,
of our continued focus on a high rising standard of living in an
era of diminishing national resources? Is our growing knowledge
of the mechanics of information processing gradually giving us
the means of persuasion against a person's will? These are just
two examples of issues which must come to the forefront rather

than being relegated to the sidelines (Engel 1981).

FUTURE EXPECTATIONS

Professor Engel clearly has been an innovator and a motivator. He has pioneered in areas such as cognitive dissonance, modeling consumer behavior and applying consumer behavior concepts to promotional strategy. He has been an innovator in the development of textbooks that properly blend theory, methodology and empirical findings, all with an emphasis on pragmatic implications. Engel has been a motivator in helping to get a relatively new discipline started and moving in the right direction.

He has been and still is a man of action.

- Many people talked about the need to develop more graduate courses in consumer behavior. While many were still talking about it, Professor Engel did it.

- Many people talked about the need for a textbook that could help teach the topic of consumer behavior. While many were still talking about it, Professor Engel did it.

- Many people talked about the need for an interdisciplinary organization that focused on the topic of consumer behavior. While many were still talking about it, Professor Engel did it.

- Many people talked about the opportunity to commit your life totally to something you really believed in. While many were still talking about it, Professor Engel did it.

- Many people talked about the need and opportunity to apply consumer behavior concepts to developing countries. While many were still talking about it, Professor Engel did it.

What can we expect from Professor Engel in the future? We believe he will continue to work hard at carrying out those things to which he has made a commitment. He will, we are certain, remain an innovator and a motivator in all that he undertakes. In his previously mentioned acceptance speech as a Fellow of Consumer Behavior, Professor Engel commented briefly about challenges and how we as a discipline need to respond to them. He stated his position and anticipated role as follows:

89

Can we rise to these challenges? Only time will
tell, but I will do my best to be a part of the solution. While I am not so visible in "mainline" circles
as I once was, this is only because of the arena in
which I work. I hope to remain as a functioning and
responsible contributor to this field for years to
come (Engel 1981).

Many times we often reach points in our career or chosen
discipline when we will ask questions like "If not us, who?
And if not now, when?" But we also need to address two additional questions in our planning. "If I am not for myself, who
will be for me? But if I am only for myself, what am I?"

We are proud to say that Professor Engel has responded
many times by saying now is the time and we are the people to
do it. At the same time he has reminded us we need to think
not only about ourselves, but also about the role we play in
the lives of our fellow colleagues and the totality of society.

Jim, we thank you very much for your twenty years of contributions to consumer behavior. We look forward to at least
twenty more. Thank you.

REFERENCES

Engel, James F. (1961), "Motivation Research, Magic or Menace,"
Part I Michigan Business Review 13 (March), pp. 28-32. Reprinted in Stuart H. Beitt (ed.), Consumer Behavior and the
Behavior Sciences (New York: John Wiley & Sons, Inc., 1966),
pp. 42-43; and in Steven J. Shaw and C. McFerron Gittinger
(eds.), Marketing in Business Management (New York: The
MacMillan Company, 1963), pp. 259-265.

_____ (1961), "Motivation Research, Magic or Menace,"
Part II Michigan Business Review 13, (May), pp. 25-28+.

_____ (1962), "Tape Recorders in Consumer Research,"
Journal of Marketing (April), pp. 73-74.

_____ (1963), "Are Automobile Purchases Dissonant Consumers?" Journal of Marketing (April), pp. 58-58. Reprinted
in Stuart H. Britt (ed.), Consumer Behavior and the Behavioral
Sciences (New York: John Wiley & Sons, Inc., 1966), pp. 546-
547.

_____ (1963), "The Psychological Consequences of a Major
Purchase Decision," in William S. Decker (ed.), Marketing in
Transition (Chicago: American Marketing Association, 1963),
pp. 462-475.

_____ (1965), "Further Pursuit of the Dissonant Consumer: A Comment," Journal of Marketing (April), pp. 33-34.

_____ (1966), "Sources of Influence in the Acceptance of New Products for Self-Medication: Preliminary Findings," in R. Haas (ed.), Science, Technology, and Marketing (Chicago: American Marketing Association), pp. 776-82.

_____ (1969), "Campus Chaos: God's Opportunity," Good News, A Forum for Scriptural Christianity within the United Methodist Church (October-December), pp. 20-23.

_____ (1977), "Great Commission or Great Commotion?" Eternity (September), p. 14.

_____ (1979), Contemporary Christian Communications: Its Theory and Practice (New York: Thomas Nelson Publishers).

_____ (1981), "The Discipline of Consumer Research: Permanent Adolescence or Maturity," in Advances in Consumer Research VIII, Kent B. Monroe (ed.), (Ann Arbor: Association for Consumer Research), pp. 12-14.

_____, Theodore N. Beckman, and William R. Davidson (1967), Marketing, Eighth edition (New York: Ronald Press Company, Inc.).

_____, Roger D. Blackwell, and David T. Kollat (1968), Consumer Behavior, (Hinsdale, IL: Dryden). Second edition 1973; Third edition, 1978; Fourth edition 1982 (with Roger D. Blackwell).

_____, M. A. Cayley, and Henry Fiorillo (1972), Market Segmentation: Concept and Applications, (New York: Holt, Rinehart, and Winston, Inc.).

_____, M. L. Dean, and W. W. Talarzyk (1972), "The Influence of Package Copy Claims on Consumer Product Evaluations," Journal of Marketing (April), pp. 34-39.

_____, Henry F. Fiorillo, and Murray A. Cayley (1971), "Segmentation: Its Place in Marketing Management," The Business Quarterly (Spring), pp. 64-75.

_____, Henry F. Fiorillo, and Murray A. Cayley (1971), "Segmentation: Prospect and Promise," The Business Quarterly (Summer), pp. 459-69.

_____, and Donald H. Granbois (1965), "The Longitudinal Approach to Studying Marketing Behavior," in Peter D.

Bennett (ed.), <u>Marketing and Economic Development</u> (Chicago: American Marketing Association), pp. 205-221.

_____, David A. Knapp, and Deanne E. Knapp (1966), "The Public, The Pharmacist, and Self-Medication," <u>Journal of the American Pharmaceutical Association</u> (September), pp. 460-462.

_____, and W. Wilbert Norton (1975), <u>What's Gone Wrong with the Harvest? A Communication Strategy for the Church and World Evangelization</u> (Grand Rapids, MI: The Zondervan Corporation) (Chinese translation by Timothy Lam, published by Christian Communications, Ltd., Hong Kong, 1980).

_____, and L. W. Stern (1965), "The Influence of Brand Preference on the Perception of Persuasion," in L. Smith (ed.), <u>Reflections on Progress in Marketing</u> (Chicago: American Marketing Association), pp. 205-221.

_____, W. Wayne Talarzyk, and Carl M. Larson (1971), <u>Cases in Promotional Strategy</u> (Homewood, IL: Richard D. Irwin, Inc.).

_____, and Hugh G. Wales (1961), "Research Interviews: An Analysis of Cartoon and Verbal Questioning," <u>Medical Marketing</u> (December), pp. 6-13.

_____, and Hugh G. Wales (1962), "Spoken Versus Pictures Questions Taboo Topics," <u>Journal of Advertising Research</u> (March), pp. 11-17.

_____, Hugh G. Wales, and Martin R. Warshaw (1967), <u>Promotional Strategy</u>, (Homewood, IL: Richard D. Irwin, Inc.). Second edition, 1971; Third edition, 1975; (with Martin Warshaw and Thomas Kinnear) Fourth edition, 1979.

_____, and Martin R. Warshaw (1963), "Linear Programming: Boon or Boondoggle?" <u>Proceedings of the 1963 American Marketing Association Public Utilities Marketing Conference</u>, pp. 30-39.

_____, and Martin R. Warshaw (1964), "Allocating Advertising Dollars by Linear Programming," <u>Journal of Advertising Research</u> (September), pp. 42-48.

Hartley, Robert F. (1974), Review of <u>Consumer Behavior</u>, Second Edition, 1973 by Engel, Kollat, and Blackwell, <u>Journal of Marketing</u>, 38, (April), p. 107.

Kassarjian, Harold H. (1981), "Presentation of the ACR Award: 'Fellow in Consumer Behavior' to John A. Howard and James F.

Engel," in Advances in Consumer Research VIII, edited by Kent
B. Monroe (Ann Arbor: Association for Consumer Research),
pp. 6-8.

Scott, Carol A. (1981), A review of six Consumer Behavior
textbooks, Journal of Marketing, 45 (Winter), pp. 160-161.

Teach, Richard D. (1969), "Macro Textbook on Micro Behavior,"
A review of Consumer Behavior, 1968 by Engel, Kollat, and
Blackwell, Journal of Marketing, 33, (April), p. 105.

CONSUMER ATTITUDES AND BEHAVIOR:
A THEORY OF REASONED ACTION

Icek Ajzen, University of Massachusetts, Amherst

Given my long-standing association with Martin Fishbein, it is perhaps only natural that I should have been asked to comment on his work and evaluate his contributions to the field of consumer behavior. There are, of course, many people who could give you a more objective assessment of Marty's work, but few would be as pleased as I am to accept this assignment. For over a dozen years now, Marty and I have worked in close collaboration, developing and testing a theory of social behavior. We have conducted joint research projects, written theoretical and empirical papers, and published two books together. Through all of these interactions, I have learned to appreciate his incisive mind, his ability to quickly expose the essential elements of a problem and to integrate seemingly diverse aspects of human behavior. His impact is felt not only in the field of social psychology, which is his professional base, but also in a variety of more applied fields, notably the area of consumer behavior. He well deserves the honor bestowed on him with the Paul D. Converse award.

Marty's early work focused on the development of attitudes. He brought to this issue a sophisticated neo-behaviorist perspective, but his orientation has over the years become much more cognitive. This work culminated in the formulation of a linear composition model that described the relation between beliefs and attitudes (Fishbein 1963), and the development of techniques to measure the model's constructs (Fishbein and Raven 1962).

I joined up with him in the very early stages of the development of what, in the marketing literature, has been called the "extended Fishbein model" and which, in our recent book (Ajzen and Fishbein 1980), we have named a "theory of reasoned action." We have described the theory and its empirical support in several places (e.g., Ajzen and Fishbein 1973, 1980; Fishbein and Ajzen 1975) and I will here provide only a brief summary to refresh your memory.

The Theory of Reasoned Action
The theory's ultimate goal is to predict and explain an individual's behavior. It makes the assumption that most behaviors of social relevance are under volitional control and, consistent with this assumption, it views a person's intention to perform (or not to perform) a behavior as the immediate

determinant of that action. Thus, barring unforeseen events, a person's intention should permit highly accurate prediction of his behavior. It should be obvious, however, that intentions can change over time; the longer the time interval, the greater the likelihood that events will occur which will produce changes in intentions. It follows that accuracy of prediction will usually decline as the time interval between measurement of intention and behavioral observation increases.

Since the theory's goal is to explain human behavior, not merely to predict it, the next step in the analysis is to identify the determinants of intentions. According to the theory of reasoned action, a person's intention is a function of two basic determinants, one personal in nature and the other reflecting social influence. The personal factor is the individual's positive or negative evaluation of performing the behavior; this factor is termed attitude toward the behavior. Note that the theory is concerned with attitudes toward behaviors and not with the more conventional attitudes toward such targets as physical objects, people, products, or institutions. The second determinant of intention is the person's perception of the social pressures put on him to perform or not perform the behavior in question. Since it deals with perceived prescriptions, this factor is termed subjective norm. Generally speaking, people will intend to perform a behavior when they evaluate it positively and when they believe that important others think they should perform it.

The theory assumes that the relative importance of attitudes and subjective norms depends in part on the intention under investigation. For some intentions, attitudinal considerations, while for other intentions normative considerations may predominate. Frequently, both factors are important determinants of the intention. In addition, the relative weights of the attitudinal and normative factors may vary from one person to another. The discussion of the theory up to this point is summarized symbolically in Equation 1, where $\underline{B}$ is the behavior of interest, $\underline{I}$ is the person's intention to perform behavior $\underline{B}$,

$$\underline{B} \sim \underline{I} = \underline{w}_1 \underline{A}_{\underline{B}} + \underline{w}_2 \underline{SN} \tag{1}$$

$\underline{A}_{\underline{B}}$ is the person's attitude toward performing behavior $\underline{B}$, $\underline{SN}$ is the person's subjective norm concerning performance of behavior $\underline{B}$, and $\underline{w}_1$ and $\underline{w}_2$ are empirically determined weighting parameters that reflect the relative importance of $\underline{A}_{\underline{B}}$ and $\underline{SN}$.

For many practical purposes, this level of explanation may be sufficient. However, for a more complete understanding of intentions it is necessary to explain why people hold certain attitudes and subjective norms. The theory of reasoned action

states that any attitude is a function of salient beliefs a-
bout the attitude object. Each belief links the object with a
valued attribute. The attitude is determined by the person's
evaluation of the attributes associated with the object and by
the strength of these associations. Specifically, the evaluation of each salient attribute contributes to the attitude in
proportion to the person's subjective probability that the object has the attribute in question. By multiplying belief
strength and attribute evaluation, and summing the resulting
products, we obtain an estimate of attitude toward an object
based on the person's salient beliefs about that object. This
information-processing theory of attitude is presented symboli-
cally in Equation 2, where $\underline{A}$ stands for attitude, $\underline{b}_i$ is the
belief (subjective probability) that the attitude object has
attribute $\underline{i}$, $\underline{e}_i$ is the evaluation of attribute $\underline{i}$, and the sum
is over the $\underline{n}$ salient beliefs. When dealing with attitude

$$\underline{A} = \sum_{\underline{i}=1}^{\underline{n}} \underline{b}_i \underline{e}_i \tag{2}$$

toward a behavior, most salient beliefs link the behavior to
positively or negatively valued outcomes. Generally speaking,
a person who believes that performing a given behavior will
lead to mostly positive outcomes will hold a favorable attitude
toward performing the behavior, while a person who believes
that performing the behavior will lead to mostly negative outcomes will hold an unfavorable attitude. The beliefs that
underlie a person's attitude toward a behavior are termed behavioral beliefs.

Subjective norms are also assumed to be a function of beliefs, but beliefs of a different kind, namely, the person's
beliefs that specific individuals or groups think he should or
should not perform the behavior. These beliefs underlying the
subjective norm are termed normative beliefs. Generally speaking, a person who believes that most referents with whom he is
motivated to comply think he should perform the behavior will
perceive social pressure to do so. Conversely, a person who
believes that most referents with whom he is motivated to comply
think he should not perform the behavior will have a subjective
norm that puts pressure on him to avoid performing the behavior.
The relation between normative beliefs and subjective norm is
expressed symbolically in Equation 3. Here, again, $\underline{SN}$ is the

$$\underline{SN} = \sum_{\underline{j}=1}^{\underline{n}} \underline{b}_j \underline{m}_j \tag{3}$$

subjective norm, $\underline{b}_j$ is the normative belief concerning referent

j, m_j is the person's motivation to comply with referent j, and $\overline{n}$ is the number of salient normative beliefs.

My discussion of the theory of reasoned action shows how behavior can be explained in terms of a limited number of concepts. Through a series of intervening steps it traces the causes of behavior back to the person's beliefs. Each successive step in this sequence from behavior to beliefs provides a more comprehensive account of the factors underlying the behavior. That is, each step represents a different level of explanation for the person's behavior. At the most global level, behavior is assumed to be determined by intention. At the next level, these intentions are themselves explained in terms of attitudes toward the behavior and subjective norms. The third level accounts for these attitudes and subjective norms in terms of beliefs about the consequences of performing the behavior and about the normative expectations of relevant referents. In the final analysis, then, a person's behavior is explained by reference to his or her beliefs; behavior is assumed to be guided by considerations concerning its likely consequences and the prescriptions of important others, hence the name, a "theory of reasoned action."

This approach differs considerably from other attempts to explain human behavior which tend to rely on such concepts as personality traits, attitudes toward people or institutions, and demographic characteristics. To be sure, variables of this kind are often found to be related to the behavior of interest. They do not, however, constitute an integral part of the theory of reasoned action. Instead, they are considered to be "external variables" that can affect behavior only indirectly by influencing the beliefs a person holds or the relative importance he attaches to attitudinal and normative considerations.

Figure 1 illustrates the theory of reasoned action and the way its constructs may mediate the effects of external variables on behavior. It is important to note, however, that there is no necessary link between any external variable and a given behavior. Some external variables may bear a relation to the behavior under investigation while others may not, and even when a relationship is discovered, it may change over time and from one population to another.

FIGURE 1

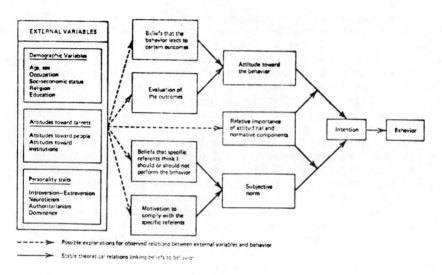

A Theory of Reasoned Action

Links to Observables: Antecedents and Consequences

Much attitude research in marketing seems to have focused
on the links between beliefs and attitudes. Various kinds of
composition and decomposition models have been tested and compared with each other. The relation between beliefs and attitudes is, however, only one concern of the theory of reasoned
action. The theory has many other important implications for
the field of consumer behavior. In the remainder, I would like
to address some issues concerning the theory's links to observ-
ables at both ends: the relations of external variables to beliefs about products or services, and the relation between buying intentions and actual purchasing behavior.

External Variables and Beliefs. As I noted earlier, the
theory of reasoned action assumes no necessary link between external variables and behavioral or normative beliefs. Consider, for example, the case of personality variables. It might
appear reasonable to argue that balding men who are low in
self-confidence (or high in social anxiety) are particularly
likely to believe that wearing a toupee would be to their advantage. On the other hand, one might also maintain that such
individuals would be easily embarrassed if it became apparent
that they are wearing a hair piece. Hence, one should not expect a simple or consistent effect of self-confidence on beliefs about wearing a toupee or on actual behavior.

There are, of course, certain external variables that may have a more stable effect on beliefs, attitudes, and behavior. For example, gender is closely linked to the use of certain commercial products: most women, but few men, use lipstick; women use perfume more than men; and men buy more cigars than women. However, even relationships of this kind can change with time as evidenced by the fact that men have started wearing fur coats and women have taken to wearing ties. Clearly, men and woman may hold different beliefs about the consequences of buying and using various products, but these differences may change or disappear over time, and they may depend on a particular cultural or subcultural milieu. The same is true of other external variables and, according to the theory of reasoned action, it is for this reason that external variables are unreliable predictors of behavior.

In the field of marketing, attitudes toward brands and products are often used to predict preferences among brands, buying intentions, and actual buying behavior. According to the theory of reasoned action, such attitudes are also external variables with no necessary relations to the determinants of consumer behavior. It is true, of course, that, in many instances, the more positive a person's attitude toward a given brand, the more favorable will be his attitude toward buying that brand. However, a strong relation between these two types of attitude cannot be taken for granted. Brand attitudes may not be strongly related to attitudes toward buying the brand in question because the salient beliefs that determine these two attitudes may differ greatly. Although beliefs about buying a certain product may involve some of the product's attributes, other consequences may also be salient. For example, a person may believe that "the Corvette is a sports car" and that "buying a Corvette is buying a sports car." However, she may also believe that "buying a Corvette will raise my insurance premium," a belief that does not refer to a product attribute and that may have little effect on the attitude toward Corvettes - although it may well have a strong effect on the attitude toward buying a Corvette.

Or, to take another example, my wife very much likes beautiful ornaments, especially precious jewels. Yet her attitude toward her buying jewelry for herself is quite negative; she believes that a woman should not have to buy her own jewelry. Thus, she is willing, and eager, to own jewelry, receive it as a gift, wear it, and admire it; her overall predisposition is positive; but she has a negative attitude toward one particular behavior, namely, buying jewelry for herself.

The difference between beliefs about a product and beliefs about buying that product is particularly obvious whenever some time or contextual element is involved. Clearly, my beliefs about "buying flowers for my secretary" are apt to be very different from my beliefs about "flowers" as such. Similarly, beliefs about "whiskey" will differ from beliefs about "drinking whiskey in the morning," and these beliefs will in turn differ from beliefs about "drinking whiskey at a party."

In a recent study (Ajzen and Fishbein 1980, Chapter 12) we obtained data that illustrates this point. Using a free response format, one group of college students was asked to list attributes they associate with Chevrolets, while a second group was asked to list their beliefs about buying a Chevrolet in the next three years. Table 1 shows the most frequently emitted

TABLE 1

Beliefs about Chevrolets and About Buying
a Chevrolet in the Next Three Years

Chevrolets are	Buying a Chevrolet in the next three years
Moderately priced	Provide transportation
Ordinary cars	Put me in financial difficulty
Well built	Lead to high upkeep costs
Dependable	Cost less now than later
Easily serviced	Lead to my paying high insurance
American made	

Adapted from Ajzen and Fishbein (1980, Chapter 12).

beliefs in each case. It can be seen that the two sets of beliefs differed greatly; beliefs about Chevrolets were concerned with product attributes such as moderate price and dependability, while beliefs about buying a Chevrolet in the next three years dealt with the consequences of this behavior, including payment of costly insurance premiums and high upkeep costs. As might be expected, these differences in beliefs produced very different attitudes toward Chevrolets and toward buying a Chevrolet in the next three years. Measures of these two attitudes were obtained by means of semantic differential scales, and the correlation between them was found to be .30.

Clearly, then, brand attitudes are not the same as attitudes toward buying the brand in question, and in many cases these two attitudes may not even be highly correlated with each other. According to the theory of reasoned action, it would be to our advantage to focus on attitudes toward buying a given product rather than on attitudes toward the product itself. There is, in fact, plenty of empirical evidence to support the claim that attitudes toward a behavior are better predicators of that behavior than are attitudes toward the target at which the behavior is directed. A major review of the relevant literature is available (Ajzen and Fishbein 1977).

Table 2 illustrates the advantage of measuring attitudes toward a behavior in the context of consumer decisions. For each of five brands of automobiles, attitudes toward buying the

TABLE 2

Prediction of Buying Intentions from Brand
Attitudes and Attitudes Toward Buying

Brand	Attitude toward the Brand	Attitude toward buying the brand
Ford	.58	.65
V.W.	.62	.74
Chevrolet	.46	.72*
Mercedes	.09	.53*
Jaguar	.00	.45*

*Significant difference ($p < .05$) between prediction based on brand attitude and on attitude toward buying.

From Ajzen and Fishbein (1980, Chapter 12).
From Ajzen and Fishbein (1980, Chapter 12).

brand predicted buying intentions among college students better than did attitudes toward the brands themselves.

Intentions and Behavior. The research just described used behavioral intentions, rather than actual behavior, as the criterion measure. Since it has been found that intentions can serve as accurate predictors of behavior, this practice has become quite common in recent years, especially in cases where it would be difficult or impossible to obtain measures of behavior. The importance of intentions in the theory of reasoned action goes, however, beyond the role they may play as convenient substitutes for behavior. Measures of behavioral intention can help us clarify the nature of the relationships between beliefs

101

and attitudes on the one hand and overt behavior on the other.

Research on the relationship between attitudes and behavior has, in recent years, shifted to an examination of variables that are assumed to moderate the strength of this relationship. It has been proposed that the strength of attitude-behavior relations is contingent on a variety of factors, including direct experience with the attitude object or with the behavior, confidence with which the attitude is held, internal consistency of the attitude, and such individual difference variables as self-monitoring and self-consciousness. Much of the research dealing with the moderating effects of these variables, however, has tended to confound correspondence between attitudes and behavior with the stability or instability of behavioral dispositions.

Consider, for example, the personality variable of self-monitoring (Snyder 1974). According to Snyder, people differ in the extent to which their behavior is susceptible to situational or interpersonal cues as opposed to inner states or dispositions. For high self-monitoring individuals, whose behavior is guided by situational cues, little correspondence is expected between attitudes and behavior. In contrast, substantial attitude-behavior correspondence is expected for low self-monitors whose behavior is guided by cues regarding internal states. Snyder has developed a scale to measure the self-monitoring trait, and empirical research has tended to support his predictions (e.g., Snyder and Swann 1976; Zanna, Olson and Fazio 1980).

In a recent statement, Snyder (in press) tried to explicate the process whereby self-monitoring affects the attitude-behavior relation. He argued that, in comparison to high self-monitoring individuals, low self-monitors are more likely to act in accordance with their attitudes because they are more aware of their attitudes and regard their attitudes as more relevant guides to action.

The theory of reasoned action suggests an alternative interpretation which focuses on the intention-behavior relationship. Although intentions are assumed to be the immediate determinants of actions, this does not mean that there will always be perfect correspondence between a measure of intention and observed behavior. Intentions are usually assessed some time prior to observation of behavior. Since intentions may change over time, the measure of intention available to the investigator may differ from actual intention at the time that the behavior is observed. Intention can thus be expected to predict behavior only if the intention has not changed prior to performance of the behavior.

By assessing behavioral intentions, in addition to attitudes and behavior, Ajzen, Timko and White (1981) were able to show that the effect of self-monitoring on the attitude-behavior relation has little to do with the attitude's perceived relevance for behavior. Instead, the effect of self-monitoring was attributable to differences in the stability of intentions.

Shortly before the 1980 presidential elections, respondents indicated their attitudes and intentions with respect to two behaviors: voting in the forthcoming election and smoking marijuana in the next three or four weeks. In addition, they completed Snyder's (1974) self-monitoring scale. About three weeks later, following the election, the respondents were recontacted and asked to report whether they had voted in the election, whether they had smoked marijuana since the last interview and, if so, how many times they had smoked marijuana.

Attitude-behavior correlations were found to be significant and, as in previous research, to be stronger for low than high self-monitors. The correlations between attitudes and intentions were also highly significant, but there were no differences between high and low self-monitors in these correlations. This suggests that low self-monitors did perceive their attitudes to be relevant to the behaviors of interest, just as much as did high self-monitors. Finally, there were marked differences between the two groups in terms of the intention-behavior correlations. Table 3 shows that these correlations were significantly stronger for low than for high self-monitors. It

TABLE 3

Intention-Behavior Correlations

Behavioral criterion	Total sample	High self-monitors	Low self-monitors
Voting	.70	.59	.82*
Smoking marijuana (yes/no)	.72	.66	.77
Smoking marijuana (No. of times)	.47	.42	.70*

*Significant difference (p<.05) between high and low self-monitors.

From Ajzen, Timko, and White (1981).

thus appears that differences in self-monitoring are related
not to the perceived relevance of attitudes to behavior but
rather to differences in people's tendencies to carry out their
behavioral intentions. The attitudes toward the behaviors examined influenced the intentions of low as well as high self-
monitoring individuals. Low self-monitors, however, were more
likely to carry out their plans than were high self-monitors.
The intentions of low self-monitors appear to be relatively un-
affected by external circumstances or events; they thus remain
relatively stable over time and permit accurate prediction of
subsequent behavior. In contrast, high self-monitors seem to be
more easily deflected by external factors; their intentions
thus change more readily; and a measure of intention obtained
at a previous point in time may not permit accurate prediction
of later behavior.

This study illustrates the value of considering behavioral
intention as a variable that mediates between attitude and behavior. Measures of intention provide estimates of behavioral
tendencies that can be obtained at the time of attitude measurement. This enables us to assess the relation between attitudes
and behavioral tendencies before the intentions have had time
to change, as well as assessing the relation of attitudes to
actual behavior at a later date. As a result, we can determine
whether low attitude-behavior correlations are to be interpreted
as evidence of intrinsically weak relationships between these
variables or as evidence for changes in behavioral dispositions.
Many decision-making models in the field of marketing link attitudes directly to consumer behavior. Although the data I have
presented were obtained in a different context, they suggest
that much can be gained by following the theory of reasoned
action and interposing intentions as a mediating construct.

CONCLUSION

In commenting on Martin Fishbein's work, I have concentrated on his theoretical contributions, although I have also
presented data to illustrate and support derivations from the
theory of reasoned action. This emphasis on theory has not
been accidental. In my view, Marty's major contributions have
been at the theoretical level. He has done much to clarify the
nature of attitudes, the way they are formed, and their relations to behavior. With the theory of reasoned action, he has
contributed to our understanding of the relationships among beliefs, attitudes, and intentions, and the ways in which these
variables may mediate the effects of other factors on behavior.
Although Marty has published many empirical papers, his commitment and devotion have been to the development of a better
theory of human behavior. In doing so he has demonstrated

104

again the validity of the saying attributed to Kurt Lewin, that "there is nothing more practical than a good theory." His efforts have produced a theory which has not only received support in controlled laboratory research, but which has also been found useful by practitioners in a variety of applied fields. We are today giving recognition to this combination of theoretical insight and practical utility that characterizes Marty's work.

REFERENCES

Ajzen, I. and M. Fishbein (1973), Attitudinal and normative variables as predictors of specific behaviors. Journal of Personality and Social Psychology, 27, 41-57.

Ajzen, I. and M. Fishbein (1977), Attitude-behavior relations: A theoretical analysis and review of empirical research. Psychological Bulletin, 84, 888-918.

Ajzen, I. and M. Fishbein (1980), Understanding attitudes and predicting social behavior, Englewood-Cliffs, NJ: Prentice-Hall.

Ajzen, I., C. Timko and J. B. White (1981), Self-monitoring and the attitude-behavior relation. Unpublished manuscript. University of Massachusetts.

Fishbein, M. (1963), An investigation of the relationships between beliefs about an object and the attitude toward that object, Human Relations, 16, 233-240.

Fishbein, M. and I. Ajzen (1975), Belief, attitude, intention, and behavior: An introduction to theory and research, Reading, MA: Addison-Wesley.

Fishbein, M. and B. H. Raven (1962), The AB scales: An operational definition of belief and attitude, Human Relations, 15, 35-44.

Snyder, M. (1974), Self-monitoring of expressive behavior, Journal of Personality and Social Psychology, 30, 526-537.

Snyder, M. When believing means doing: Creating links between attitudes and behavior. In M. P. Zanna, C. P. Herman and E. T. Higgins (Eds.), Variability and consistency in social behavior: The Ontario Symposium, Vol. 2, Hillsdale, NJ: Erlbaum, in press.

Snyder, M. and W. B. Swann, Jr. (1976), When actions reflect attitudes: The politics of impression management. Journal of Personality and Social Psychology, 34, 1034-1042.

Zanna, M. P., J. M. Olson and R. H. Fazio (1980), Attitude-behavior consistency: An individual difference perspective. Journal of Personality and Social Psychology, 38, 432-440.

LESSONS LEARNED FROM A DECADE OF
MULTIATTRIBUTE ATTITUDE RESEARCH IN MARKETING

Richard J. Lutz, University of California

INTRODUCTION

The decade of the 1970's was characterized by an enormous amount of marketing research devoted to testing and applying a general class of multiattribute attitude models. Initiated with a focus on consumer brand choice behavior, this stream of research gradually expanded its horizons to include questions related to almost every aspect of marketing decision-making, with the result that a multiattribute perspective is now pervasive, indeed virtually inescapable, in modern marketing research and practice.

The purpose of the present paper is to (1) trace the origins of multiattribute attitude research in marketing, with particular attention being devoted to the role of Professor Martin Fishbein; (2) to summarize what has been learned from this research in terms of measurement, theory, and application; and (3) to suggest some possible avenues for further multiattribute research in marketing.

ORIGINS

Any faithful reader of the marketing literature over the past ten years will instantly recognize the following formula:

$$A_o = \sum_{i=1}^{N} B_i a_i \qquad (1)$$

where A_o is <u>attitude</u> toward some object; B_i is the <u>strength of</u> belief that the object is associated with some other concept; a_i is the <u>evaluative aspect</u>, or evaluation, of the associated concept; and N is the number of <u>salient</u> associated concepts (Fishbein 1963). While this formula did not find its way into the marketing literature until the very late 1960's, it is safe to say that it appeared literally hundreds of times during the 1970's.

What accounts for this explosion of research? What led marketing researchers and practitioners alike to embrace the multiattribute attitude model with such unprecedented fervor?

Why does multiattribute research continue to abound in a literature previously characterized by an endless stream of fads?

Upon reflection, it seems clear that the rather substantial impact which Professor Fishbein's work has had in marketing is in large part due to the fact that his theory, as represented algebraically in Eqn. 1, provided a theoretical framework which directly supported what by the late 1960's had become axiomatic in marketing. By axiomatic is meant a fundamental assumption about the nature of the field. Perhaps the best characterization of this axiom can be found in Kotler's (1967) text:

> "Therefore we shall find it useful to define a product as: a bundle of physical, service, and symbolic particulars expected to yield satisfactions or benefits to the buyer" (p. 289).

Note that the above statement is designed to be a definition of a product, i.e., the entity which is to be marketed. Definitions are inherently axiomatic; they cannot be subjected to empirical test. A close inspection of the definition of product reveals its basic multiattribute nature. Substitution of the word "attributes" for "particulars" makes the point very clear. Thus, it can be asserted that the very foundation of marketing rests on a multiattribute conception of the core concept, i.e., the product. Fishbein's theory, offering a convenient and readily operationalized multiattribute framework, was thus rapidly adopted due to its immediate relevance to this central tenet of marketing thought.

The utility of the multiattribute approach was enhanced by concurrent developments in marketing theory. In 1969, Kotler and Levy first suggested a broadened marketing concept, which Kotler (1972) later refined into his generic conceptualization of marketing. Subsequent research into generic marketing issues over the ensuing ten years has been surpassed in quantity only by research on the multiattribute model. A key feature of the generic concept of marketing is its focus on the exchange (Bagozzi 1975, 1978, 1979) as the unit of analysis. Since what is being exchanged, at the most generic level, are sets of values, benefits or satisfactions, the multiattribute model is quite convenient as a means of analyzing the components of any marketing exchange.

Because many of the exchanges analyzed under the rubric of generic or broadened marketing involve services rather than products, and most do not entail the transfer of a monetary consideration, this expansion of marketing's domain has forced marketing scientists to analyze the traditional "product" from a perspective more consistent with Kotler's (1967) definition, which has already been shown to incorporate multiattribute notions. Hence, the development of the generic marketing concept virtually simultaneously with the investigation of multiattribute models in marketing appears to have been a major factor in fostering the enormous interest in the topic.

Fishbein's attitude theory, which was readily translatable into a multiattribute model of product and brand attitudes, served as a major catalyst in the inception of marketing multi-attribute research. However, there were other early contributors who were also partially responsible for this stream of research. Certainly the work of social psychologist Milton Rosenberg (1956) was a major contributing force; much of the early multiattribute research in marketing identified its conceptual base as "the Fishbein-Rosenberg model." Howard and Sheth's (1969) influential Theory of Buyer Behavior incorporated an attitude construct which was causally dependent on choice criteria (i.e., attributes). Their work explicitly noted the similarity of their conception to those of Fishbein and Rosenberg.

Several initial exploratory investigations of the multiattribute model were reported at various conferences in 1969 and 1970. Perhaps most significant were presentations made at what turned out to be the first conference of the fledgling Association for Consumer Research in 1969 and at the 1970 conference on attitude research held at the University of Illinois. It was at the latter conference where Fishbein first presented his viewpoint face-to-face with marketing attitude researchers.

In his 1972 Consumer Choice Behavior: A Cognitive Theory, Flemming Hansen emphasized an attribute-based choice model, relying heavily on Fishbein's and Rosenberg's work. The first Journal of Marketing Research articles on the subject also appeared in 1972 (Bass and Talarzyk 1972 and Sheth and Talarzyk 1972). The final early contribution to be mentioned here was the Wilkie and Pessemier (1973) review of approximately 40 marketing multiattribute studies. Their paper was to become one of the most-cited articles of the 1970's, and it was extremely influential in spawning the plethora of studies on the multiattribute model.

While virtually all of the early multiattribute research can be characterized as consumer behavior research, subsequent investigations have addressed a variety of managerial research issues, most notably advertising, segmentation, and new product development. Most of the current multiattribute research lies in the managerial domain. As the scope of multiattribute research has broadened from consumer behavior, so has the range of alternative formulations which have been utilized. In fact, very little current multiattribute research uses the Fishbein model per se. Rather, the multiattribute concept is what has pervaded the literature. Fishbein's work provided the initial impetus to a research stream which has flowed in many directions. Much of the remainder of this paper will deal with what has been learned, in general, from multiattribute research in marketing. And although most of the research to be cited is not strictly Fishbeinian, its roots are nevertheless found in his writings.

MULTIATTRIBUTE LESSONS LEARNED

The remainder of this treatise will focus on the contributions to knowledge which have resulted from multiattribute research in marketing. These contributions are organized into three general categories: measurement, theory, and application. The first category, measurement, refers primarily to what has been learned about multiattribute models per se, with particular attention paid to various alternative formulations. The theory and application sections will deal with the contributions of multiattribute research to the broader domains of marketing theory and practice.

Measurement
This section will attempt to provide an overview of what has been learned about the measurement of the various multiattribute model constructs. As is apparent from Eqn. 1, there are five separate issues to be treated, and this section will be organized around those: salience, belief strength (B_i), evaluative aspect (a_i), the combination rule, and the dependent variable (A_o).

Salience. A basic tenet of Fishbein's theory is that only those aspects of an attitude object which are salient are to be regarded as determinants of attitude. Measuring non-salient attributes is expected to increase error variance, and worse, may contribute to fallacious inferences regarding the cognitive basis of the attitude in question. Procedures for identifying salient attributes have not been well articulated, and a variety of approaches are evident in the literature: consumer focus groups, depth interviews, consumer listing procedures, managerial opinion, previous literature, and researcher intuition. Attempts to formalize the determination of salience (e.g. Ryan and Etzel 1976; Olson and Muderrisoglu 1979) have, for the most part, only served to underscore the problem of accurately determining salience.

At best, salience remains an elusive concept which is
expected to vary individually and situationally, though few
multiattribute studies have assessed the degree of such variation. Recent research on salience in cognitive social psychology (e.g., Taylor and Fiske 1978) suggests that salience,
as a "top of the head" phenomenon, (1) is extremely important
in influencing human judgmental processes and (2) is heavily
influenced by the situation in which the judgment is made.
Taylor and Fiske conclude on the basis of their review of
numerous studies that "...making almost any cognition...salient
will influence the subjects' attitudes and behavior" (p. 251).
This statement has significant implications for marketing researchers using the multiattribute model; if the set of salient
attributes can be varied almost at will, then past determinants
of attitude assume much less importance than prospective future
determinants.

For example, most marketing research has focused on product
attributes rather than concentrating on a broader range of
possibly salient associations. Movement from the original
attitude-toward-the-object (A_o) concept to the more behaviorally
relevant attitude-toward-the-behavior (A_B) (Fishbein and Ajzen
1975) has partially corrected for the product attribute bias,
but not fully. Consider the situation wherein the consumer is
exposed to a particularly entertaining or (obnoxious) commercial for a brand. In that case, it may be reasonable to expect
that a newly salient cognition is developed: "Brand X sponsors
interesting commercials." This non-product attribute may contribute significantly to brand attitude in that situation, but
past marketing applications of the model would mitigate against
such a cognition being identified for measurement. In short,
more work is clearly necessary in order for researchers to
have sufficient confidence that they are measuring the "correct"
set of salient attributes.

Belief strength. In the Fishbein model, belief strength
refers to the likelihood that the attitude object in question
is related to some other object or concept. In marketing, as
noted above, the related "object" has been treated as a product
or brand attribute. However, there has been a fair degree of
controversy over the appropriate delineation of product attributes; specifically, there is a difference between the amount
of some attribute possessed by a brand and the probability
that the brand possesses that amount of that attribute (Ahtola
1975). Stated another way, likelihood of possession does not
equal degree of possession. Various forms of the general
multiattribute model incorporate a number of different belief
strength measures, with the result that researchers must take
care to use the model which best suits their purpose.

Another important distinction regarding the belief
strength construct is that between <u>features</u> and <u>benefits</u>. Product features are attributes of the product per se (e.g.,
amount of fluoride in a toothpaste), while product benefits are
the expected consequences of using the product (e.g., degree
of decay prevention). Fishbein and Ajzen's (1975, 1980) Theory
of Reasoned Action makes a strong case for perceived consequences (i.e., benefits) rather than features as the building
blocks of attitude-toward-the-behavior (such as purchase
behavior). The issue of how product features are translated
into perceived product benefits is, in itself, an important
area of research. Initial work in this arena is summarized by
Neslin (1981).

Regardless of the exact nature of the belief measure used
in any particular application of the multiattribute model,
there is a persistent measurement problem which has to come to
be identified as the <u>halo effect</u> (Beckwith and Lehmann 1975).
Essentially, the halo effect phenomenon describes the tendency
for individuals to exhibit low within-brand variance in their
ratings across a number of attribute dimensions. If they hold
the brand in high regard, they tend to rate it highly on all
dimensions, and vice versa.

The halo effect is troublesome for the diagnostic utility
of the multiattribute model, since its diagnostic application
relies on a flow of causation from attribute perceptions to
attitude, rather than vice versa. The halo effect represents
a "reverse" causal flow from overall attitudinal affect to
specific attribute perceptions. Diagnoses for attitude change
strategies based on "haloed" ratings are misleading at best.
Successful application of the model, then, rests on the ability
of the researcher to tap "true" underlying perceptions; this
is a tricky task, as haloed perceptions are very real to the
people providing the ratings. The issue is whether these
cognitions are modifiable through attribute information, or
whether another approach would be necessary to induce attitude
change.

<u>Evaluative aspect</u>. Perhaps the most confusing construct
in the multiattribute model (at least in its adoption by marketing researchers), the evaluative aspect of an attribute is
its goodness or badness, in effect a "mini-attitude" toward
the attribute. Numerous papers devoted to the confusion surrounding this construct have, for the most part, succeeded in
contributing even more confusion. It may be easier to identify
what the evaluative aspect is <u>not</u> rather than what it is. It
is not <u>salience</u>; nor is it <u>importance</u> or <u>determinance</u>. It is
not a standardized regression coefficient or a derived utility
function. And it is not <u>satisfaction-dissatisfaction</u>. All of

the preceding concepts have been used by various researchers, much the same as numerous belief strength concepts have appeared in the literature. The only resonable conclusion which can be reached regarding Fishbein's evaluative aspect is that it represents a general class of "weighting" terms, the most appropriate form of which varies with the particular application at hand.

One issue with regard to the measurement of attribute "weights" which seems to be moving toward some sort of consensus is that indirect measurement such as that offered by conjoint analysis is superior to direct self-reported weights. Academic researchers and practitioners alike have recognized the demand characteristics associated with direct measurement-- another form of halo effect, it would appear, in that weights may be overstated for attributes possessed by favored brands and understated for attributes not possessed by favored brands.

Additional support for the increasing reliance on indirect measurement comes from recent research in cognitive social psychology which suggests that people are generally incapable of accurately reporting internal cognitive processes (e.g., Nisbett and Wilson 1977). Instead, people are likely to report what they think should have been going on inside their heads. The basic problem is óne of conscious awareness of the weighting process used. It is simply more difficult for people to report how important some attribute is than it is for them to report how some brand rates on that attribute. Similarly, it is not a very difficult task for consumers to report their overall attitude toward a brand. Indirect measures of attribute weights rely on these more easily retrieved brand attribute perceptions and brand attitudes, and hence appear to offer more reliable and valid measures of the weights in question.

Combination rule. The term combination rule refers to the way in which cognitive elements (i.e., beliefs and weights) are presumably "combined" mentally by consumers to yield overall judgments (e.g., attitude, intention). In the case of the Fishbein formulation, the combination rule is deterministic, with beliefs and weights combining first multiplicatively, and then additively, to yield overall attitude.

While initial applications of the multiattribute model in marketing were often labeled as investigations of consumer "information processing," it is clear now that multiattribute research may in some sense provide a measure of decision structures (Lutz 1979b) but not decision processes. Numerous alternative combination rules (e.g., conjunctive, disjunctive, linear, lexicographic) have the same property of being "structure in search of process." At this juncture, no one believes

113

that consumers really think in the way implied by these models, but the various formulations are regarded as reasonable "paramorphic" representations of decision processes (Wright 1973).

With regard to the Fishbein formulation, there is a nagging scale property problem. The mathematical operation of multiplication requires cardinal numbers, or true ratio scaled data. However, the belief strength and evaluative aspect measures are interval scales (at best) which permit transformations of the form $a+bx$. Application of these transformations to B_i and a_i measures would result in dramatically fluctuating correlations between attitude and the cognitive structure index. Fishbein and his associates have consistently recommended bipolar coding for both the belief and evaluation components, and Bettman, Capon and Lutz (1975) have provided some evidence that people do tend to respond to those scales in bipolar fashion. Nevertheless, the scaling issue is one which should not be ignored by researchers using the original Fishbein formulation. Models which rely on statistical estimation of weights are less afflicted with this problem, since interval data are permissible in most cases.

The dependent measure. Fishbein's original model specified attitude-toward-the-object, an affective dimension, as its dependent variable. In subsequent work on the Theory of Reasoned Action, Fishbein and Ajzen (1975, 1980) have articulated an attitude-toward-the-behavior construct, which is also affective in character. In marketing, a much broader array of dependent measure has been employed; intentions, preferences, behavioroid measures (e.g., the dollarmetric approach), and actual brand choice behavior. While any one of these measures may be usefully employed, it is critical to recognize the differences among the various alternatives and to select that measure which is most appropriate for the particular problem under investigation.

From a theoretical perspective, however, it should be noted that Fishbein's multiattribute work has been based on solely attitudinal (i.e., affective) variables. Use of other forms of dependent measures by marketing researchers should be justified on the basis of theoretical work other than the standard Fishbein formulation.

Summary and conclusions. As should be apparent from the foregoing discussion, there are numerous difficulties with the multiattribute model as a measure of attitude. Questionable procedures for determining salience, widely varying conceptions and measurement of beliefs and weights, and questionable mathematical operations given scale properties, combine to lead to the conclusion that the multiattribute model is inferior to

114

other attitude measurement models. Semantic differential, Likert and Thurstone scales all exhibit better reliability and convergent validity.

But the real contribution of the multiattribute model lies not in the measurement arena, but rather in its theoretical statement regarding the relationship between the cognitive and affective domains. We turn our attention to the theoretical contributions of multiattribute research in the next section.

Theory

The primary reason why the multiattribute model has received so much attention in marketing is the presumed explanatory power it offers. In particular, the theory underlying multiattribute research specifies a causal relationship flowing from cognitive structure to attitude. This relationship is the basis for the multiattribute model's claim to diagnostic ability, a feature of considerable importance to marketers.

However, as noted earlier, the presence of a measurement halo effect as well as notions of affective-cognitive consistency (Rosenberg 1956) suggest that causation may also flow from attitude to cognitive structure. That is, a person's overall feelings toward a brand may govern his or her ratings of the brand on key attributes, thus bringing perceptions into line with affect. Some (e.g., Zajonc 1980) would argue that this "reverse" flow of causation is more common than the cognition-to-affect flow suggested by the multiattribute model; obviously, it is extraordinarily difficult to sort out, empirically, the actual flow of causation in any particular instance. Most likely, there is a constant two-way flow between cognition and affect.

For multiattribute theory to be useful, it is not essential that cognition-to-affect be the only causal flow of significance. Rather, it is only necessary that cognition-to-affect be supported as a significant causal relationship in its own right. That is, the absolute magnitude of the postulated relationship is more critical than its magnitude relative to the affect-to-cognition flow of effects.

Most attempts aimed at verifying the multiattribute model have relied on correlational tests (Wilkie and Pessemier 1973, Lutz and Bettman 1977), which are incapable of establishing causal relationships. However, a number of studies have investigated the model in an attitude change context (e.g., Lutz 1975, 1977; Mazis and Adkinson 1976; Olson and Dover 1978; Holbrook 1978). In all cases, there has been strong evidence for the hypothesized causal flows: changing belief strength leads to a change in attitude; changing the weighting term leads to attitude change.

Viewed from a metatheoretical perspective, the large number of correlational studies, together with the smaller number of attitude change studies, can be considered attempts to falsify multiattribute theory's key proposition. That is, failure to observe significant correlations between affect and cognition and, more importantly, failure to find attitude change following belief or evaluation change, would have cast doubt on the truth of the underlying theory. Such falsification has not occurred; multiattribute theory has proven to be quite robust, withstanding literally hundreds of falsification attempts.

Based on the weight of the evidence, it is suggested that we have established a "law" of marketing behavior. That is, multiattribute theory's basic proposition is no longer just a hypothesis to be tested, but rather stands as an empirically verified relationship which has become ingrained in modern marketing thought (as shall be seen in the Application section of this paper).

Stated formally, the Law of Multiattribute-Based Market Response holds that:

A consumer's attitudinal and behavioral responses to any market offering are a function of the salient perceived consequences to the consumer of purchasing that offering and the desirability of those consequences to the consumer.

Several points in the formal statement bear some explanation. First, both attitudinal and behavioral responses by consumers are seen as causally dependent on attribute perceptions and weights. This is consistent with the role generally ascribed to attitude as a mediating causal variable in many theories of human behavior (e.g., Fishbein and Ajzen 1975). And, despite past concerns over weak attitude-behavior relationships, recent research has begun to establish more clearly a significant causal role for attitude in the determination of behavior (e.g., Bentler and Speckart 1979).

Second, the term market offering is used to denote the total array of controllable marketing stimuli surrounding a product. Thus, a market offering consists of not just the brand, but the brand, as packaged, priced, promoted and distributed. The particular configuration of these cues which is encountered by a consumer at any point in time is the determinant of the consumer's response. This expanded conception of the market offering provides a useful basis for explaining short-run responses (say, to special sales promotions) which a focus on the brand only would not. Consideration of the total configuration impinging on the consumer at a point in time also draws attention to the notion of salient consequences ranging over time and situations, a critical point which has been overlooked in many marketing applications.

Third, the general term consequences is used rather than attributes, which too often connotes product features, or benefits, which connotes positive aspects of the market offering. Some consequences of purchase are not necessarily desirable, most notably the expenditure of money. Other possible negative consequences could be conceived as well--e.g., buying, and thus supporting, a brand that airs obnoxious television commercials, or supporting a brand produced by a company with a poor environmental protection record. It should be noted that this consequences construct is basically the same as the one espoused by Fishbein and Ajzen (1975, 1980) as the underlying determinant of attitude. The difference here is that all salient perceived consequences are considered as determinants of attitude, while Fishbein and Ajzen break out social consequences as determinants of their social norm construct but not of attitude, a theoretical position which has come under recent attack (e.g., Ryan 1977; Miniard and Cohen 1979).

Fourth, the weighting term in the Law of Multiattribute-Based Market Response is represented as a desirability construct. Desirability is basically an affective dimension, ranging from positive to negative, and hence is quite consistent with Fishbein's evaluative aspect or the general notions of valence, utility, and satisfaction.

It is asserted here that the general proposition as stated above has received ample empirical support, resulting in general acceptance by marketing scholars and practitioners. As such, then, the proposition has achieved the status of a law of marketing. As pointed out by Hunt (1976), marketing laws, like those in other social science disciplines, are not of the deductive-nomological variety often found in the physical sciences, but rather are of the inductive-statistical type. That is, there is a probabilistic relationship between the explanans (i.e., consequences and their desirability) and the explanandum (i.e., consumer response). Such laws are only weakly falsifiable and rest on the "total evidence" available (Hunt 1976, p. 35). It is argued here that the total evidence in support of the Law of Multiattribute-Based Market Response is extremely impressive. As shall be seen in the last section of this paper, this law forms the basis for marketing decision-making in a wide variety of contexts.

117

Implications for research. Given the widespread acceptance of the Law of Multiattribute-Based Market Response, at
least implicitly if not under the label suggested here, it is
apparent that research attention should be focused on gaining
a fuller understanding of the multiattribute model's components.
That is, we need to move our understanding of market response
a level deeper by attempting to answer such questions as:
What are the determinants of the perception of consequences?
What causes a consequence to become salient? What are the
determinants of consequence desirability? Issues regarding
interactions among consequences, inferential processes, the
role of more central values, and the impact of marketing
controllable variables need to be addressed.

Application

Multiattribute principles have found their way into virtually every area of marketing research and managerial decision-
making. Obviously, the impact on consumer behavior research
has been enormous, but multiattribute concepts also form the
underpinning of approaches to such "managerial" problems as
pricing, segmentation, and new product development. Table 1
displays a list of areas in which multiattribute concepts have
been employed along with representative articles to which the
interested reader can turn for further information. Practically
the only area of marketing which is not represented in Table 1
is distribution. An admittedly less than thorough search
failed to locate any recent article dealing with a multiattribute analysis of distribution decisions. However, the old
notions of marketing, through the distribution process, creating
time and place utilities seem quite consistent with a multiattribute conception. Additionally, two attributes which appear
to be salient in a number of situations are prestige and
convenience, both of which are traditionally thought to be
related to the alternative distribution strategies, exclusive
and intensive, respectively.

TABLE 1

AREAS IN WHICH MULTIATTRIBUTE CONCEPTS HAVE BEEN APPLIED

Consumer Behavior (e.g., Lutz and Bettman 1976)
Advertising Strategy (e.g., Boyd, Ray and Strong 1972)
Personal Selling Strategy (e.g., Weitz 1978)
Product Positioning (e.g., Urban 1975)
Benefit Segmentation (e.g., Calantone and Sawyer 1978)
New Product Development (e.g., Shocker and Srinivasan 1979)
Pricing (e.g., Shapiro and Jackson 1978)
Concept Testing (e.g., Wind 1973)
Advertising Pretesting (e.g., Lutz 1979a)
Sales Forecasting (e.g., Warshaw 1980)

In reading the more applied articles utilizing multi-attribute notions, one is struck by the degree to which the multi-attribute foundation is simply taken as a given. There is, little doubt in the authors' minds, apparently, about the appropriateness of the multiattribute approach. Other issues are debated and analyzed, but the multiattribute foundation is axiomatic, reflecting the generality of the Law of Multiattribute-Based Market Response.

CONCLUSION

In conclusion, it is clear that the multiattribute conception of attitude has had an enormous impact on modern marketing thought. The current generation of marketing students is being taught that a multiattribute analysis of virtually any marketing problem is at least one, if not the, fundamental approach to finding an effective solution. Martin Fishbein's work provided a solid theoretical framework for this crystalization of multiattribute notions in the field of marketing, and it is obvious that we owe him an enormous intellectual debt.

REFERENCES

Ahtola, Olli T. (1975), "The Vector Model of Preferences: An Alternative to the Fishbein Model", Journal of Marketing Research, 12, 52-9.

Bagozzi, Richard P. (1975), "Marketing as Exchange", Journal of Marketing, 39, 32-9.

_____ (1978), "Marketing as Exchange: A Theory of Transactions in the Marketplace", American Behavioral Scientists, 21, 535-56.

_____ (1979), "Toward a Formal Theory of Marketing Exchanges", in O.C. Ferrell, S.W. Brown and C.W. Lamb, Jr., eds., Conceptual and Theoretical Developments in Marketing, Chicago: American Marketing Association, 431-47.

Bass, Frank M., and W. Wayne Talarzyk (1972), "An Attitude Model for the Study of Brand Preference", Journal of Marketing Research, 9, 93-6.

Beckwith, Neil E., and Donald R. Lehmann (1975), "The Importance of Halo Effects in Multiattribute Attitude Models", Journal of Marketing Research, 12, 265-75.

Bentler, P.M., and George Speckart (1979), "Models of Attitude-Behavior Relations", Psychological Review, 86, 452-64.

Bettman, James, R., Noel Capon, and Richard J. Lutz (1975), "Cognitive Algebra in Multiattribute Attitude Models", Journal of Marketing Research, 12, 151-64.

Boyd, Harper W., Michael L. Ray, and Edward C. Strong (1972), "An Attitudinal Framework for Advertising Strategy", Journal of Marketing, 36, 27-33.

Calantone, Roger J., and Alan G. Sawyer (1978), "The Stability of Benefit Segments", Journal of Marketing Research, 15, 395-404.

Fishbein, Martin (1963), "An Investigation of the Relationships between Beliefs about an Object and the Attitude toward that Object", Human Relations, 16, 233-9.

_____ (1980), "A Theory of Reasoned Action: Some Applications and Implications", in H.E. Howe, Jr., and M.M. Page, eds., Nebraska Symposium on Motivation 1979: Beliefs, Attitudes, and Values, Lincoln: University of Nebraska Press, 65-116.

_____, and Icek Ajzen (1975), Belief, Attitude, Intention, and Behavior: An Introduction to Theory and Research, Reading: Massachusetts: Addison-Wesley.

Hansen, Flemming (1972), Consumer Choice Behavior: A Cognitive Theory, New York: Free Press.

Holbrook, Morris B. (1978), "Beyond Attitude Structure: Toward the Information Determinants of Attitude", Journal of Marketing Research, 15, 545-56.

Howard, John A., and Jagdish N. Sheth (1969), The Theory of Buyer Behavior, New York: Wiley.

Hunt, Shelby D. (1976), Marketing Theory: Conceptual Foundations of Research in Marketing, Columbus, Ohio: Grid.

Kotler, Philip (1967), Marketing Management: Analysis, Planning, and Control, Englewood Cliffs, New Jersey: Prentice-Hall.

_____ (1972), "A Generic Concept of Marketing", Journal of Marketing, 36, 46-54.

_____, and Sidney J. Levy (1969), "Broadening the Concept of Marketing", Journal of Marketing, 33, 10-5.

Lutz, Richard J. (1975), "Changing Brand Attitudes through Modification of Cognitive Structure", Journal of Consumer Research, 1, 49-59.

_____ (1977), "An Experimental Investigation of Causal Relations Among Cognitions, Affect, and Behavioral Intentions", Journal of Consumer Research, 3, 197-208.

_____ (1979a), "A Functional Theory Framework for Designing and Pretesting Advertising Themes", in J.C. Maloney and B. Silverman, eds., Attitude Research Plays for High Stakes, Chicago: American Marketing Association, 37-49.

_____ (1979b), "How Difficult Is It to Change Consumer Decision Structures?", in A.D. Shocker, ed., Analytic Approaches to Product and Marketing Planning, Cambridge, Massachusetts: Marketing Science Institute, 317-34.

_____, and James R. Bettman (1977), "Multiattribute Models in Marketing: A Bicentennial Review", in A.G. Woodside, J.N. Sheth, and P.D. Bennett, eds., Consumer and Industrial Buying Behavior, New York: Elsevier, 137-50.

Mazis, Michael B., and Janice E. Adkinson (1976), "An Experimental Evaluation of a Proposed Corrective Advertising Remedy", Journal of Marketing Research, 12, 178-83.

Miniard, Paul W., and Joel B. Cohen (1979), "Isolating Attitudinal and Normative Influences in Behavioral Intentions Models", Journal of Marketing Research, 16, 102-10.

Neslin, Scott A. (1981), "Linking Product Features to Perceptions: Self-Stated Versus Statiscally Revealed Importance Weights", Journal of Marketing Research, 18, 73-9.

Nisbett, Richard E., and Timothy D. Wilson (1977), "Telling More Than We Know: Verbal Reports About Mental Processes", Psychological Review, 84, 231-59.

Olson, Jerry C., and Philip A. Dover (1978), "Cognitive Effects of Deceptive Advertising", Journal of Marketing Research, 15 29-38.

Olson, Jerry C., and Aydin Muderrisoglu (1979), "The Stability of Responses Obtained by Free Elicitations: Implications for Measuring Attritute Salience and Memory Structure", in W.W. Wilkie, ed., Advances in Consumer Research, Vol. VI, Ann Arbor: Association for Consumer Research, 269-75.

Rosenberg, Milton J. (1956), "Cognitive Structure and Attitudinal Affect", Journal of Abnormal and Social Psychology, 53, 367-72.

Ryan, Michael J. (1977), "Programmatic Research Based on Fishbein's Extended Model", in A.G. Woodside, J.N. Sheth, and P.D. Bennett, eds., Consumer and Industrial Buying Behavior, New York: Elsevier, 151-66.

_____, and Michael J. Etzel (1976), "The Nature of Salient Outcomes and Referents in the Extended Model", in B.B. Anderson, ed., Advances in Consumer Research, Vol. III, Cincinnati: Association for Consumer Research, 485-90.

Shapiro, Benson P., and Barbara B. Jackson (1978), "Industrial Pricing to Meet Customer Needs", Harvard Business Review 56, 199-27.

Sheth, Jagdish N., and W. Wayne Talarzyk (1972), "Perceived Instrumentality and Value Importance as Determinants of Attitudes", Journal of Marketing Research, 9, 6-9.

Shocker, Allan D., and V. Srinivasan (1979), "Multiattribute Approaches for Product Concept Evaluation and Generation: A Critical Review", Journal of Marketing Research, 16, 159-80.

Taylor, Shelley E., and Susan T. Fiske (1978), "Salience, Attention, and Attribution: Top of the Head Phenomena", in L. Berkowitz, ed., Advances in Experimental Social Psychology, Vol. 11, New York: Academic Press, 249-88.

Urban, Glen (1975), "PERCEPTOR" A Model for Product Positioning", Management Science, 21, 858-71.

Warshaw, Paul R. (1980), "A New Model for Predicting Behavioral Intentions: An Alternative to Fishbein", Journal of Marketing Research, 17, 153-72.

Weitz, Barton A. (1978), "Relationship Between Salesperson Performance and Understanding of Customer Decision Making", Journal of Marketing Research, 15, 501-16.

Wilkie, William L., and Edgar A. Pessemier (1973), "Issues in Marketing's Use of Multi-Attribute Attitude Models", Journal of Marketing Research, 10, 428-41.

Wind, Yoram (1973), "A New Procedure for Concept Evaluation", Journal of Marketing, 37, 2-11.

Wright, Peter (1974), "Research Orientations for Analysing Consumer Judgment Strategies", in S. Ward and P. Wright, eds., <u>Advances in Consumer Research</u>, Vol. I., Urbana, Illinois: Association for Consumer Research, 268-79.

Zajonc, Robert B. (1980), "Preferences Need No Inferences", <u>American Psychologist</u>, 15, 151-75.